T0171644

Kingdom Warming

Sheila Kelly, Author

Order this book online at www.trafford.com
or email orders@trafford.com

Most Trafford titles are also available at major online book retailers.

Printed in the United States of America.

ISBN: 978-1-4269-8189-0 (sc)
ISBN: 978-1-4269-8190-6 (e)

Trafford rev. 01/26/2012

 www.trafford.com

North America & international
toll-free: 1 888 232 4444 (USA & Canada)
phone: 250 383 6864 ♦ fax: 812 355 4082

Kingdom Warming

Unless otherwise identified, all scripture quotations are from King James Version of the Bible.

Uttermost Ministries, Inc.
P.O. Box 340734
Jamaica, New York 11434
347 878 5290
Email - uttermostministries@gmail.com
Website - www.uttermostministriesinc.com

Editing
To The Uttermost, Inc.
Cover Art
To The Uttermost, Inc.
Photography
Wilma Lewis

Table of Contents

Acknowledgements

I acknowledge the endless support of my parents Elder Ivory Kelly and Shepherd Mother Mary Kelly and my siblings, Andre', Monica and Le Var Kelly.

I certainly would like to recognize the Adams Family for their support and faithfulness to this ministry.

I also acknowledge Bishop Joseph N. Williams for his continued prayers, encouragement, and trust in my ministry.

FORWARD

Amazing are the revelatory writers as they explain things through
their lenses of perception that are easily seen, but not to others. I
have written many forwards but I am most proud to be a part of this
particular release. This work is not for the faint hearted, nor for the
casual reader, but it is thought provoking as Dr. Kelly takes the time
to explain in vivid detail the activities concerning the extraordinary
happenings unbeknownst to many in the Kingdom of God.

When we hear the phrase "Global Warming" it only brings to mind a
negative connotation, but God knows what He is doing and we know
that all things work together for the good. Many of the tragic natural
disasters, the meaningless loss of life and noticeable changes in our
local and global weather patterns, can be attributed to the affects of
Global warming. Between the pages of "Kingdom Warming" you
will find the parallel demonstrated, using the kingdoms of this world
vs. the Kingdoms of our Christ, is uncanny. Dr. Kelly reveals that the
coexistence of these two kingdoms, are in fact, experiencing many
of the same happenings. *"Howbeit...first...that which is natural; and
afterward that which is spiritual."* 1 Corinthians 15:46

In these compact chapters, you will begin to understand that these
natural occurrences and changes are necessary ingredients for the
release of many of the unfulfilled spiritual promises and prophecies of
God, toward His people.

The Right Reverend
Liston Page II., M. Div.
Senior Pastor, The Highway Church, Paterson, NJ
2nd Vice Presiding Prelate
Greater Highway Deliverance Ministries Inc.

FORWARD

"But it is not the spiritual life which came first, but the physical and then the spiritual." 1 Corinthians 15:46 Amp

From the beginning, God established many processes of cleaning, elimination and safety measures keeping the earth habitable for His creation. However, this system of checks and balances were superseded by the greed of man, causing what we understand today as Global warming. The development of environmental agencies became necessary to help educate and find ways to lower the level of pollution that has been released into the atmosphere. Likewise, many Christians do not understand that they are responsible for the shape that their Spiritual atmosphere is in. Pollution in the Spirit realm has been caused by previous generations that still remain today. This pollution is now coupled with the effects of various works of the flesh that have in turn released additional pollutants by many present day Christians.

"Kingdom Warming" is theologically sound and prophetically relevant to the present condition of the Body of Christ, explaining first the natural and then the spiritual aspects of "Kingdom Warming" happening today. Dr. Kelly uses many subjects including earth & living science, biology, meteorology, agriculture, and other areas to help explain the events taking place in the Spiritual atmosphere. The vast education and knowledge of study of eschatology, the study of the end times, has afforded the foundation of inspiration that comes forth on these pages with many profound revelations.

"Kingdom Warming" is recommended for those who are Kingdom minded; those who understand Kingdom Principles yet seeing the increase of another law at work. As long as Christ delays His coming, Christians will need to live in the Kingdom of God on this earth. Let this manuscript become a guide that will compel and show the believer the importance of becoming spiritual environmental agents, ready to maintain the Spiritual balance in the Kingdom, until His return. Matthews 28:19-20.

Dr. LeVar R. Kelly, B.S., B.R.E., M.R.E., D.R.E.
Author of The FAITH Reaction,
& Founder of Var Ministries

Preface

"Now we have received, not the spirit of the world, but the spirit which is of God; that we might know the things that are freely given to us of God." I Corinthians 2:12

"It is the glory of God to conceal a thing: but the honor of kings is to search out a matter. The heaven for height, and the earth for depth..." Proverbs 25:2-3a

There are some things that are freely revealed when we receive the power of the Holy Spirit. But, as we are also a chosen generation, royal priests and kings of the Most High, there is another level of wealth, knowledge and power that can be afforded to us. It would be our good pleasure to take honor in searching out the mysteries of the heavens and the earth. For in these elements we can discover the glories that God would have us uncover concerning His creation in the heavens, the earth and they that dwell therein. Psalms 24:1

When we begin to use words like conceal, search, mystery and reveal, we cannot help but think of the word revelation, which in turn make us think of the last book in the Bible, the book of Revelation. Another word that may come to mind that describes the Book of Revelation is the Greek word apocalypse. It means "lifting of the veil" or "to reveal." These are terms used that pertain to the disclosure of information to certain privileged persons, things that are hidden from the majority of humankind. The mystery of the word apocalypse is somewhat like the veil of parables used in the teachings of Christ. They were earthly stories with hidden spiritual or heavenly meanings. Today, the meaning of apocalypse is all too often used to refer to the end of the world.

As I write this book, I'm forever reminded to thank God for His gift of salvation that moved me from the kingdom of darkness into the Kingdom of Light. For as far back as I can remember, I was always captivated by the mystical, mysterious cloaking of dark mysteries and sentences. I was raised in a saved Christian household, so almost naturally, I was drawn to the mysteries of the unknown, cloaked or veiled things of the scriptures. During my days of searching and reading the book of Revelation, I realized not many Christians or preachers seemed to tackle these seemingly veiled scriptures in their conversations, nor were they ready to give an answer concerning its interpretation.

As for me concerning the last days and the prophetic stuff, it was always fascinating and extremely motivating tackling the mysteries of God. When I was younger, I remember writing in composition notebooks concerning my interpretations of the different characters and events within the book of Revelation. One thing was for sure, as I interviewed the different possibilities of interpretations, from Moses, from the prophets, from the sayings of Christ and His disciples; the imminent return of the King of Glory was and is still evident.

As we encounter the fulfillment and the unveiling of *"the Revelation of Jesus Christ, which God gave unto Him, to show us His servants things which must shortly come to pass"* Revelation 1:1, we will begin to discover that many of the hidden revelations have and will be revealed in the events of heavens and on the earth.

The study of our natural heaven, the atmosphere and its phenomena has been given to the science of Meteorology. The Greek word, meteorology means "high in the sky." This study involves interdisciplinary factors that involve researchers, students, and teachers having the same goal of connecting and integrating several academic schools of thought, professions and technologies. Their pursuit is of one task, to predict what's coming, it's affects on plants and animals, preservation of the earth and what measures should be taken at any given time.

A meteorologist is an individual with specialized education, who using proven scientific principles can explain, observe and forecast our earth's atmospheric phenomena. They can also help us understand the atmospheric effects and life on the planet. Their goal and task involves gathering data from the almanac, noting the different temperature trends, the ever changing seasons, air pressure and water vapor from the troposphere, all aiding in understanding the climate changes. From the assimilation of this data the meteorologist becomes skillful in observing, predicting or forecasting the earth's atmospheric phenomena. This also, makes them qualified in making conclusions concerning the atmospheric effects on the earth, animals and plant life.

If understanding the natural atmosphere around us with its uncertain skies, over lapping seasons and uncommon weather phenomenon's, helps to predict the behavior for the day, week and seasons within the regions around us, then just maybe, the employment of the meteorologist in the Kingdom of God could likewise bring about understanding of its changing seasons, climate variations, weather patterns and warming effects that may influence the life and future of all in its province.

This planet is not our home nor do we belong to the kingdoms of this world Revelation 11:15 as we see the fulfillment of Luke 21:11. It describes earthquakes in divers places, famines, pestilences; fearful sights and great signs that shall come on the earth from heaven. However, Jesus said that the Kingdom of God cometh not with observation, for you cannot see it with the natural eye but the Kingdom of God is within us. Luke 17:20-22 We belong to the Kingdom of God and are looking for a new heaven and a new earth, for the first heaven and the first earth shall pass away Revelation 21:1 but, while we are here let's become spiritual mad scientist willing to search, dig and compile data of the changing spiritual climate occurring within the Kingdom of God.

Knowing that all truth is parallel, we consider 1 Corinthians 15:46 that says, *"Howbeit that was not first which is spiritual, but that which is natural; and afterward that which is spiritual."* Let's look at the many paralleling effects of the undeniable data of Global Warming on this earth as it too may be occurring in the Kingdom of God.

Introduction

An ecologist observes the behavior of the bluebirds,

The geologist exams the distribution of fossils,

A chemist observes the rate of chemical reactions at various temperatures and pressures,

A biologist observes the reactions of tissue in the presence of various stimulants,

The meteorologist is one that studies the atmosphere and focuses on weather.

Their main focus is to forecast weather conditions.

Variables that exist in the earth's atmosphere are determined by temperature, air pressure, water vapor and the interactions of each of these. The majority of Earth's observed weather is located in the lowest part of earth's atmospheric layer called the troposphere. Meteorology is important as it affects many diverse fields such as the military, transportation, agriculture, construction and everyday life.

Can you predict the weather by looking at the color of the clouds or by observing the behavior of animals? Many small communities believe that they can still predict floods, storms and droughts the traditional way -- by tracking nature. The Vietnamese farmers and their fishermen believe that if the dragonfly flies high in the sky, it will be a sunny day but if it flies low there will be rain. Although, many of these and other predictions were passed down orally or kept alive through proverbs, folk songs and legends, it's a wonder if any of it holds some truth. These old folk legends have since been recorded by a group of weather agencies in the Southeast Asian country. The goal of the agency is to determine whether these stories still or ever held any truth with regard to weather change and climate prediction.

However, for many of us living in the USA, when waking up in the morning the second thing reached for after turning off the alarm clock is the remote control to check our preferred weather channel. Your local weather station is the ultimate and probably your best source of weather information. Various weather persons can deliver hour by hour or morning, afternoon and evening weather conditions. The technology of weather predictions have advanced greatly to the point that your favorite weather person can even give you a 5 day or 7 day forecast. The prediction of local, national or international weather helps us plan daily and weekly activities from playing outdoor tennis, rescheduling the weekend beach party or whether to expect flight delays. Knowing the daily weather around us can help us decide the best garments for the day, the places to visit or the proper equipment that may be needed such as an umbrella, boots or wool scarf.

Contrary to the sci-fi movies with all the high tech and digital imaging, the weather is not something that man can control. They can however affect the atmosphere by what is done on the earth, to the earth and around the earth, but man cannot control the weather. So, it becomes very important that we understand how to protect and conduct ourselves in different weather situations, as we maneuver through it, planning life with minimum interruptions, because life goes on.

Likewise, as citizens of the Kingdom where God is the King, there too are regions, laws, systems and weather patterns. It would be wise to understand the relative climate of the place we live. When relocating because of employment, for example, weather and climate are taken into consideration. As the born again transfers from the kingdom of darkness into the Kingdom of Light, they likewise, should begin to equally understand the weather patterns, conditions and seasons within the Kingdom of God.

Understanding Kingdom weather, climate and the different seasonal changes are important as they affect the life or death of our planted seed(s). It is our responsibility to protect and multiply what has been planted within. In these last of the last days, we cannot afford the plan, the Word, the gifts or fruit in our lives to succumb to a wipe out, being washed up or carried away due to the rapid weather changes happening right before our eyes within the Kingdom of God.

It is amazing how we study other planets, solar systems, come to the aid of other countries and their wars, but no one seems to take an interest in the undisputed climate changes happening within the Kingdom of God. Our entire earth as we know it today is experiencing what is called Global Warming. Global Warming is occurring because of human behavior and their activities. Let us now consider the behavior and activities surrounding the Kingdom dwellers as they too may be the direct result of "Kingdom Warming."

Chapter I
In the Beginning

In the beginning God created the heaven and the earth.
Genesis 1:1

In His recreation of the earth, the Creator announced what He felt about the creation of each day created.

On the first day God said, *Let there be light...and it was good.*

On the third day God said, *Let the waters under the heaven be gathered together unto one place, and let the dry land appear...and it was good.*

On the fourth day God said, *Let there be lights in the firmament of the heaven to divide the day from the night; and let them be for signs, and for seasons, and for days, and years: And let them be for lights in the firmament of the heaven to give light upon the earth... and it was good.*

On the fifth day God said, *Let the waters bring forth abundantly the moving creature that hath life, and fowl that may fly above the earth in the open firmament of heaven ...and it was good.*

On the sixth day God said, *Let us make man in our image, after our likeness: and let them have dominion over the fish of the sea, and over the fowl of the air, and over the cattle, and over all the earth, and over every creeping thing that creepeth upon the earth ...and it was <u>very</u> good.*

Have you noticed that on days 1,3,4,5 and 6 God announced the creation of those days and the things created on those days as good? Well, what was created on the second day? Genesis 1:6-8 is where we find the creation of the second day. *"And God said, Let there be a firmament in the midst of the waters, and let it divide the waters from the waters. And God made the firmament, and divided the waters which were under the firmament from the waters which were above the firmament: and it was <u>so</u>. And God called the firmament Heaven. And the evening and the morning were the second day."*

It is generally believed that between Genesis 1:1 and Genesis 1:2 that there was some type of catastrophe that took place on the earth as a result of lucifer's expulsion from the lofty position given to him in heaven. Verse one says, *"In the beginning God made the heaven and the earth."* This heaven and earth sounds complete having form, vegetation and inhabitants. Then verse two says, *"And the earth was without form and void, and darkness covered the face of the deep."* The question is raised: What happened that the completed heaven and earth of verse one is now seen without form, void and covered in darkness, in verse two?

On the second day of creation the firmament was made by God. The word firmament is found in the King James Version of scripture 17 times and in every instance of its Hebraic meaning remained constant. Its meaning states that our earth's firmament is a wide, a visible arching canopy of the sky or atmosphere that is located over our heads. This arched canopy is mentioned by King David in Psalm 19:1 who also states that, *"The heavens declare the glory of God; and the firmament sheweth His handy work."*

It is through scripture and the science of man that we recognize the firmament consists of three levels. The first level contains the clouds, stars, sun and moon. The second level contains the outer space, its planets, galaxies and Milky Ways. And the third level is where God dwells. The Apostle Paul tries to convey the span of the firmament by comparing it to the eternal love of God in Ephesians 3:17-19. It says, *"That Christ may dwell in your hearts by faith; that ye, being rooted and grounded in love, may be able to comprehend with all saints what is the breadth, and length, and depth, and height; and to know the love of Christ"*...which is everlasting to everlasting as He is.

The purpose of this infinite firmament, that the Creator so wisely created between the heaven and the earth, was to separate the waters from the waters of the earth and the waters of the heavens in preparation of His crowning glory, which is man.

Again, most theologians teach that between Genesis 1:1 and Genesis 1:2, between the finished heaven and earth and then the earth seen without form and void was the result of lucifer's cast down from heaven. Lucifer, the son of the morning lost his brightness as the result of his rebellion against the Most High. And because there is no rebellion or darkness in heaven, there was no place for him or the one-third of the innumerable host of heaven that followed him, they were casted into outer darkness. This experience was like a type of hell as he was propelled into a place without the presence of God. Any place without God is and should be considered a place of hell and darkness.

John 1:4-5 says, *"In Him was Life; and the Life was the Light of men. And the Light shineth in darkness; and the darkness comprehended it not."* Also 1 John 1:5 is quoted, *"This then is the message which we have heard of Him, and declare unto you, that God is Light, and in Him is no darkness at all."* Let's be aware that darkness cannot comprehend light and when the two meet, darkness must flee from the room, the area or the space as soon as the switch is thrown. Darkness must leave as fast as lightning flashes from the east to the west and as fast as the speed of light. Jesus speaks of the meeting of Light with darkness, as the rebellious lucifer meets the face of God. In Luke 10:18 Jesus is quoted saying, *"I beheld satan as lightning fall from heaven."* Jesus here is speaking of the past and future final end of satan as he encountered the Light of God. At the end of the world as we know it, satan will have experienced several cast downs and encounters with the Light of God. His first encounter was seen as he revolted in heaven and is believed to have caused the earth's plunge into the description of the world seen in Geneses 1:2.

But as we ponder again at the accolades of the second day...there was none. Therefore, it is safe to conclude that there were no accolades given to the 2nd day because at the completion of it, satan took up space and residents between the space of access and communication between God and Man, which is within the firmament.

The Kingdom of God started in heaven. The Kingdom of God expanded to the earth. The Kingdom of God was planted Eastward in a Garden called Eden. It was in Eden He planted the man and the woman, His crowning glory. God's purpose for man on the earth was to establish and expand His Kingdom as free willed agents. In Eden they were to live, move and have their being in His domain. They were in relationship with their Creator. They were given authority, responsibility and were informed of their duties. Genesis 2:15 says, *"And the LORD God took the man, and put him into the Garden of Eden to dress it and to keep it."* Adam was to guard and to keep the Kingdom of God on the earth.

"To dress it" is to bring about a level of coverage that would come from having a position of supervision, maintenance and management. "To dress it" we understand that they were to provide optimum conditions for themselves, the animals, the parcel of land provided and everything connected to these things, which includes the firmament. "To dress it" means to till the ground, producing optimum conditions for everything in it to flourish, grow and reproduce seed after its own kind. "To dress it" also included providing optimum conditions for the inhabitants that were assigned to the Garden. The plan of God can be seen in Psalm 72:18-20, *"Blessed be the LORD God, the God of Israel, Who only does wondrous things! And blessed be His glorious name forever! And let the whole earth be filled with His glory. Amen and Amen."* The purpose of man was to take what God had given: dominion, family, skill and talents along with the law of God and grow the whole earth, filling it with His glory. It is interesting to see that God had also given man proper dress for the posture, "To dress it."

The Kingdom of God is the place where He reigns and rules. The Kingdom of God is the place where His people live in relationship with Him and each other, doing things His way. In the Kingdom of God, His people have ownership and responsibility. They work the land that takes care of the family, the animal kingdom and all things connected. In the Kingdom of God it is the job of His people to work it, grow it and keep it.

Until now, the Kingdom of God has not changed, there is no difference. The Kingdom of God can still be experienced. God still reigns and rules. His people are in relationship with Him. They have a mind to obey and to work. They seek to maintain family by working the land together. They still have dominion over the fish, fowl, beast and every creepy thing and the responsibility to maintain optimum balance and conditions for their kingdoms. It is still the charge of man to advance, establish and experience the Kingdom of God. Likewise, in this dispensation of grace, the Kingdom mind-set of God's people is to remain dressed to work, to grow and to keep the Kingdom of God, until the whole earth is filled with His Glory.

But unlike Adam who was unaware of the invisible, unseen and increasing activities in the firmament, we are not ignorant.

Chapter II
In the End

Now satan, this self proclaimed "prince of the air," at the creation of the firmament is able to go to and fro in the earth and above the earth. He was able to have an audience with God in Job 1:6 he was able to walk about seeking whom he may devour in 1 Peter 5:8 and he was able to cause fire and great wind down from heaven in Job 1:16, 18.

The enemy released chaos in the place that lies between the space of heaven and earth called principalities, stratosphere and firmament. At the fall of man, the enemy was allowed to release chaos in the place that lies in the space between the body and spirit called the soul. This self proclaimed "prince of the air," "prince of this world," and "ruler of the kingdom of the air," is the same spirit that is now at work in the sons of disobedience. Ephesians 2:1-2 The firmament and the souls of men were two distinctive places designed exclusively for the inhabitant of the Spirit of God only and not that of the enemy.

And it is time for the church to drive old satan away. That is why we need more than ever intercessors, believers who will stand in the gap! We say to all the apostles, prophets, evangelist, preachers and teachers you can still hold these titles but add the heart and the spirit of an intercessor to it. Become an apostolic intercessor, a prophetic intercessor, an evangelical intercessor, etc, ready to stand on the turf of the enemy and take back the territory he has invaded.

In days gone by, the old mothers of the church may not have been theologically right about everything but one thing was for sure, they understood that prayers and answers had to get through. To have communication with God there must be a clear pathway or conduit for exchange. They would testify during testimony service and at the close of their testimony they would say, "If you know the worth of prayer and can get a prayer through, please pray my strength in the Lord, *in these last and evil days.*"

When you pick up your home or cell phone to place a call and a busy signal is heard, you're not concerned to know why, all you know is you couldn't get through! With all the power of technology it's annoying not being able to get through. Likewise, it doesn't matter where you may be on the earth; it may be in the belly of a large fish, in the inner cell of a jail or in the pit of the earth, but what concerns you most when you are in trouble, is knowing that God can receive your unhindered prayers and can release unhindered answers for your situations. It is important that your prayer have power, fight and stamina to get through the plethora of spiritual wickedness in high places. (Ephesians 6:12)

Adam was given responsibility, dominion, a family and the law of God in the Garden. He was told not only "to dress it" but "to keep it." Again, Genesis 2:15 it says, *"And the LORD God took the man, and put him into the Garden of Eden to dress it and to keep it."* "To keep it" means "to guard it." It was Adam's job to take precaution, to protect and to supervise the lot that God had given to him. "To guard it" as a military term, it means to protect or shield against. "To guard it" in the sports arena means to defend, having the ability to resist. "To guard it" is a Greek phrase that compiles these definitions in the word Shama. Shama means to brood over, protect, to stand as a guard, to defend as a shield, and to defend like a mother hen over her unborn chicks.

It is interesting that the Bible doesn't inform us if Adam was told, asked about or if he consciously knew about his "evil resident" neighbor of the air. Adam may have not known how the enemy would attack or approach, but it would have been in his best interest to look in every direction, ready to attack anything or situation that did not look like or sound pro Kingdom.

It is evident that God and man were in covenant relationship and it is also evident that man was in relationship with the animal kingdom, seeing that Adam named them all. Genesis 2:19 The enemy used the most subtle beast of the field, the serpent, to do his dirty work of deception. Genesis 3:1

SIDE BAR: Could it be that certain characters attract certain spirits or are certain spirits attracted to certain characters? It's just a question.

The serpent began to unknowingly force the children of God to stop using their Kingdom mind-set, causing them to use their human mind-set which is the soulish man. When you, Kingdom dwellers, begin to think outside of the mind-set of the Spirit of God that is within you, you have in fact entered the soulish realm of man. When Adam and Eve allowed the enemy to get their spiritual eyes off the things of God they became spiritually blind. However, the eyes of their soulish counterparts became alive and opened to soulish vision, hence the quote, "And the eyes of them both were opened." Genesis 3:7 If the enemy can get you to think outside of the Spirit of God that is within you, you have just been divided or separated from the will of God. For you to say that you are in fellowship with God, there can be no other thoughts but His, no other mind-set but His nor is there any another way but His. His ways are passed finding out, and for certain we cannot figure out God without God. The enemy caused them to look at themselves, taking their eyes off God. There are grave consequences when you take your eyes off God. James 1:14, 15 says, *"But every man is tempted, when he is drawn away of his own lust, and enticed. Then when lust hath conceived, it bringeth forth sin: and sin, when it is finished, bringeth forth death."* If man would, *"But seek ye (or see) first the kingdom of God, and His righteousness, all things shall be added."* Matthew 6:33

Kingdom dwellers are required to maintain the mind-set of the Kingdom of God by:

- Believing the Word of God
- Obeying the law of God
- Guarding the laws of God
- Guarding the Word spoken over their life
- Guarding their faith in God
- Becoming a fervent apologetic of the hope that lies within, which is God

From the beginning and until now, our purpose is still to guard and keep the Kingdom of God. We must use our weapon on praise, worship and Kingdom principles and everything else that has been given to us to form a shield against the wiles of the enemy, for "the thief cometh not, but for to steal, and to kill, and to destroy." John 10:10 What Adam failed to realize was that he was also to guard and cover his mind. It is our responsibility to cover our soulish man as it is still the place that satan wants to invade. It is the place where the will is determined. It is the place that decides our heart and actions. The enemy seeks to blind and block every mind and pathway that would keep men's souls away from the light of the truth of God. 2 Corinthians 4:4 It was the intent of the enemy from the beginning and it is the intent of the enemy today to come as a thief "but for to steal, and to kill, and to destroy..." John 10:10 He wants to steal the position and dress that we were given, he wants to kill the Spirit of God that's within us and he wants to destroy the relationship with the Father we had from the beginning. In the end, it is our responsibility to **GUARD the Kingdom of God by actively keeping the enemy out of the stratosphere of our minds and guard eternal life!**

Chapter III
Free Will
Free Will part I

Who determines the choices of men?

There are a number of handed down arguments and misconceptions lurking around the definition concerning Free will. Many philosophers have argued, taught or written volumes of discourses stating their views concerning Free will. Erasmus believes man has Free will synergistically with God. Hence the phrase, "God helps those that help themselves." Luther believes God is the force behind all man's choices and only the omnipotent God has absolute Free will. Augustine believes that man has total Free will but not apart from his natural nature. Free will disagreements may be based on theories of desires, self-mastery, values or even the omnipotence of God, but the bottom line will always come down to your choice, your will. It will be to either choose left or right, in or out, here or there, on or off and most importantly life or death.

God in His wisdom has always set before His creatures a choice. From His Word we understand that He has always allowed His creatures the freedom and power of choice. To attempt to address the many facets of Free will, as it has many dimensions is very trying. But from a Christian's point of view in relationship to the sovereignty of God, the basic and traditional definition for the purpose of this chapter of Free will is this:

- Having the ability to freely choose one of several possible alternatives based on one's own will
- Having the ability to make human choices that have not been predetermined or preordained by God
- Having the ability to make decisions the outcome of which is and cannot be known in advance by anyone

God created lucifer, a creature of Free will. He was the anointed cherub. He was covered with every precious stone and gold, and he was created having tabrets and pipes prepared in him. He was with God on the mountain of God and even in the Garden of Eden. He was perfect, until iniquity was found in him causing him to desire the position of God. Ezekiel 28:12-15 God created lucifer, son of the morning, but lucifer chose to make a conscience decision against the will of God when he declared in Isaiah 14:12-16, *"I will ascend into heaven, I will exalt my throne above the stars of God: I will sit also upon the mount of the congregation, in the sides of the north: I will ascend above the heights of the clouds; I will be like the most High."* He willed against the will of God and was brought down to hell, the pit.

Christ too, who was all man on the earth and was always God demonstrates His admission of Free will. When He was in the Garden called Gethsemane, He prayed to the Father saying, *"O my Father, if it be possible, let this cup pass from me: nevertheless not as I will, but as thou wilt."* Matthew 26:39

Adam was likewise created having free will. We understand this to be so when he was given a commandment saying, *"Of every tree of the Garden thou mayest freely eat: But of the tree of the knowledge of good and evil, thou shalt not eat of it: for in the day that thou eatest thereof thou shalt surely die."* (Genesis 2:16, 17) When the law or the laws of God have been presented, there are now choices to be made and sides to be chosen. The choice is to either believe the enforcer or not; to obey or not; to love God and His laws or not.

God wants us to choose Him and His ways. God wants Free will obedience, Free will worship and Free will praise. If we were controlled simply by the will of God and not by our own choices or decision making, then we would be nothing more than glorified puppets or robots. What God wants are willing servants! Adam, the first Free will man was given a choice. Christ, the 2nd Adam was given a choice. You are given a choice.

Who or what will determine your choice? Choose ye this day!!!

Chapter IV
Horticulture

Throughout scripture we see God has a green thumb of some sorts. Many pages from Genesis to Revelation give us a glimpse of God's steadfastness for gardening, planting and reproduction. He was the first farmer, an occupation that must be noble, worthy and Godly. *"He planted a garden eastward in Eden; and there he put the man whom he had formed. And out of the ground made the LORD God to grow every tree that is pleasant to the sight, and good for food."* Genesis 2:8, 9a

Horticulture is defined as the process of preparing soil for the purpose of raising and cultivating a small plot to medium size garden for beauty, hobby or family consumption. Agriculture refers to the practice of farming a large portion of land producing only one or two crops for profit. Putting these two arts together, Horticulture and Agriculture will reveal the art or science of cultivating fruits, flowers, and vegetables for specific human purposes.

While planting and growing is the main intent of the sower or farmer, this occupation also includes protecting the area from the elements, various pests, weeds and animals.

Horticulture also contains an unspoken language of settling down and permanency. When God planted man in the Garden, He expected man to grow, multiply; stay put, and work everything within his dominion. God expects the many varieties of seeds in His Garden to multiply in mass quantity...until the whole earth is replenished. Genesis 1:28

Horticultural and Agricultural terms are plentiful in scripture. Just to list a few:

And Jesus said unto him, No man, having put his hand to the plough, and looking back, is fit for the kingdom of God. Luke 9:62

Whose fan is in his hand, and he will thoroughly purge his floor, and gather his wheat into the garner; but he will burn up the chaff with unquenchable fire. Matthew 3:12

I am the vine, ye are the branches: He that abideth in me, and I in him, the same bringeth forth much fruit: for without Me ye can do nothing. John 12:5

Now learn a parable of the fig tree; When his branch is yet tender, and putteth forth leaves, ye know that summer is nigh. Matthew 24:32

These farming terms were also used as symbols by the prophets and their writings. Activities that Jesus often describes in His parables were often taken from the trade or science of Horticulture. As Jesus used these terminologies in His parables it brought vivid, graspable images to His listeners.

Added to the art of Horticulture is the mention of trees numerous times throughout the scriptures. From the foundation of creation trees were used literally, figuratively, and symbolically. Let's look at a few.

The Fig tree was first seen in the Garden of Eden. Its leaves were used to make aprons to cover the nakedness of Adam and Eve. Down through time the Fig tree has since become quite a noble tree and one of great importance. This tree was always connected to the wealth, health and economy of the children of Israel based on their obedience to Jehovah. Jeremiah 8:12-14

The Gophar tree is only seen during the building of Noah's ark. *"And God said unto Noah, The end of all flesh is come before me; for the earth is filled with violence through them; and, behold, I will destroy them with the earth. Make thee an ark of gopher wood; rooms shalt thou make in the ark, and shalt pitch it within and without with pitch."* Genesis 6:13-14

The Olive tree was and is still considered one of the oldest and the Holiest tree of the Holy Land. Often, the Olive tree represented new beginnings; therefore it was against the law to cut down this tree. Every aspect of this tree symbolizes something of great significance. The branches of this tree represented peace, its fruit represents productivity and the wood of this tree was used in the construction of articles for the Temple. The cherubim and the door in Solomon's Temple were made of Olive wood. This brief description of the Olive tree brings another level of meaning when we contemplate the Dove that appeared with the Olive branch in the window of Noah's ark.

It symbolized that the earth was now at peace, it was now time for productivity and ready for reconstruction. Genesis 8:11

The Acacia tree, also called Shittim is considered one of the major woods of the Bible as it was the primary wood used in the construction of the Tabernacle of Moses and its furniture. *Exodus 25:1-5 says, "And the LORD spake unto Moses, saying, Speak unto the children of Israel, that they bring me an offering: of every man that giveth it willingly with his heart ye shall take my offering. And this is the offering which ye shall take of them; gold, and silver, and brass, and blue, and purple, and scarlet, and fine linen, and goats' hair, and rams' skins dyed red, and badgers' skins, and Shittim wood."* Moses was instructed to use Shittim wood and to over laid it within and without with gold. This wood represents the humanity of man and humanity requires the covering of God seen as the over lay of gold.

Trees in scripture have been known to symbolize men. There was one incident of a blind man who encountered Jesus Christ. What is interesting to me is that this man was not blind from birth as the blind man in John 9:1. It reads, *"And as Jesus passed by, he saw a man which was blind from his birth"...to show forth the glory of God.* But this man at the healing touch of Jesus was to show some other significance. For when Jesus came to Bethsaida; they brought a blind man unto him, and besought Him to touch him. *"And He took the blind man by the hand, and led him out of the town; and when He had spit on his eyes, and put his hands upon him, He asked him if he saw ought. And he looked up, and said, I see men as trees, walking. After that He put his hands again upon his eyes, and made him look up: and he was restored, and saw every man clearly."* Mark 8:22-25 Trees with their uplifted branches are seen to God as always in a position of praise having potential of producing good fruit. Just maybe this man was given a glimpse of how God sees His praisers and worshippers. Perhaps the people around the blind man were so ready and standing in a position of praise with up lifted hands in anticipation of the miracle they were about to witness, just maybe this is what the once blind man saw and perceived as trees walking.

There are many other literal and symbolic representations of trees in scripture, but as we look at the trees of our day it is heart breaking to see how man has not valued what seems very important to our Creator. Trees are one of the most important aspects of the planet we live in. *Deuteronomy 20:19-20 says, "When thou shalt besiege a city a long time, in making war against it to take it, thou shalt not destroy the trees thereof by forcing an axe against them: for thou mayest eat of them, and thou shalt not cut them down, for the tree of the field is man's life...Only the trees which thou knowest that they be not trees for meat, thou shalt destroy and cut them down."*

Trees are vitally important to the environment, animals, and of course mankind. Living trees are not to be cut down as they bring life. Trees do matter as they increase property value and add beauty to our streets and parks. Trees matter to the earth because they filter the air, relieve asthma, skin cancer and stress related illnesses. Trees matter because they create jobs in the lumber industry that provide materials for our everyday living. Trees help to cool the atmosphere in the summer and they absorb carbon dioxide that reduces Global warming and pollution from the air. Trees of a forest matter because they create a home for over 90% of all living organisms and support wildlife that cannot be found or live anywhere else. Without trees of the forest extinction is inevitable for many species. Trees of a rainforest can provide something as insignificant as the spices for food and as important as the life giving, life prolonging and curing medicines that are used daily.

Some of the most obvious value that come from trees are its fruit, nuts, berries, syrups, dyes, fibers and latexes. In addition, the aforementioned of these few trees, give us some awareness concerning all that trees bring to the entire Globe. Our concerns for the rapid deforesting of the earth's trees should be very crucial and of great importance to all of us.

What is meant by deforesting? Deforestation is the clearance of naturally occurring forests mostly by the hand of humans. Deforesting occurs due to many things, such as: logging, for fuel, real estate, conversion of land for agriculture, for roads and highway building and by fire. Deforesting is a direct contributor and link to Global warming.

If we check the history of past landscaping we would see that almost half of the United States, three-quarters of Canada, almost all of Europe and much of the world were originally areas of forest. Today trees have been or are being cut down at such an increasing and alarming rate that if this is not stopped many unfavorable side effects could result.

You may not be aware but deforestation is also a cause of many of the global happenings on the earth. To name a few, deforestation causes:

- an increase in tick infestation
- a 50% to 100% decrease in species of animals are being lost each day
- increased soil exposed to the sun causing it to become dry and then infertile
- an increase of the earth's temperature, carbon dioxide and the destruction of the Ozone layer
- less game hunting as their habitats are being destroyed
- flooding during heavy rains as the decrease number of trees no longer have the capability to absorb large quantities of rain water

But, there are a number of ways to prevent or slow down the effects of deforestation. One way is to plant trees, perhaps plant one in your yard. New York City has adopted the "MillionTreesNYC" program. This program has an ambitious goal to plant and care for one million new trees across the City's five boroughs over the next decade. By planting one million trees, New York City can increase its urban forest thereby increasing the quality-of-life that comes with planting trees. By replacing older trees and lifeless trees, you are replenishing God's earth.

Protect the trees! Recycle newspaper, boxes and books to decrease the need for the destruction of trees. Bring awareness of the laws that would protect the forest. It only takes a few hours to destroy or burn up or chop down the wood, but it takes years to grow just one!

If men are seen as trees in the Kingdom of God, then what are the strategies in place to preserve or maintain the forest of praisers against the spirit of deforesting?

Chapter V
Trees in the Midst

Free Will part 2

The first two trees mentioned in scripture are the Tree of Life and the Tree of the Knowledge of Good and Evil. Genesis 2:9, 3:22 Have you seen their fruit?

Genesis 2:8-17 "And the LORD God planted a garden eastward in Eden; and there He put the man whom He had formed. And out of the ground made the LORD God to grow every tree that is pleasant to the sight, and good for food; the tree of life also in the midst of the garden, and the tree of knowledge of good and evil. And a river went out of Eden to water the garden; and from thence it was parted, and became into four heads. The name of the first is Pison: that is it which compasseth the whole land of Havilah, where there is gold; And the gold of that land is good: there is bdellium and the onyx stone. And the name of the second river is Gihon: the same is it that compasseth the whole land of Ethiopia. And the name of the third river is Hiddekel: that is it which go toward the east of Assyria. And the fourth river is Euphrates. And the LORD God took the man, and put him into the Garden of Eden to dress it and to keep it. And the LORD God commanded the man, saying, Of every tree of the garden thou mayest freely eat: But of the tree of the knowledge of good and evil, thou shalt not eat of it: for in the day that thou eatest thereof thou shalt surely die."

Tree of Life is mentioned throughout the scriptures: 1-*She (wisdom) is a tree of life to them that lay hold upon her: and happy is every one that retaineth her. Proverbs 3:18 2-The fruit of the righteous is a tree of life; and he that winneth souls is wise. Proverbs 11:30 3-Hope deferred maketh the heart sick: but when the desire cometh, it is a tree of life. Proverbs 13:12 4-A wholesome tongue is a tree of life: but perverseness therein is a breach in the spirit. Proverbs 15:4 5-Blessed are they that do his commandments, that they may have right to the* **tree** *of* **life***, and may enter in through the gates into the city. Revelation 22:14* So we know without a shadow of doubt that it is still in existence today, in heaven.

SIDE BAR: From the 5 above verse, do you realize that those who live to have a right to **the** tree of life have likewise grown into trees of life on the earth, seed after its own kind?

The Tree of Life was first introduced to us in the Book of Genesis as we see it in the midst of the Garden, but its description is found in the Book of Revelation. *He that hath an ear let him hear what the Spirit saith unto the churches; To him that overcometh will I give to eat of the tree of life, which is in the midst of the paradise of God. Revelation 2:7 In the midst of the street of heaven, and on either side of the river, was there the tree of life, which bare twelve manner of fruits, and yielded her fruit every month: and the leaves of the tree were for the healing of the nations. Revelation 22:2 Blessed are they that do his commandments, that they may have right to the tree of life, and may enter in through the gates into the city. Revelation 22:14*

The Tree of Life was one of the many trees Adam was allowed to eat from. It's amazing to me how many believe that he did not eat of this tree when making the statement that "Adam should have eaten from the Tree of Life." Firstly, where the Bible stops we should stop. The scriptures never said whether or not Adam ever ate from that tree. However, I believe that he did. The Tree of Life was there to regenerate his body and soul that were still one and strengthen his Spirit.

Let us compare the following 3 scriptures and their context for illumination. What is the final correlation between the Tree of Life and fruit of the Spirit? Let's read and compare the following verses:

1. *The fruit of the righteous is a tree of life; and he that winneth souls is wise.* **Proverbs 11:30**
2. *For the fruit of the Spirit is in all goodness and righteousness and truth.* **Ephesians 5:9**
3. *But the fruit of the Spirit is love, joy, peace, longsuffering, gentleness, goodness, faith, meekness, temperance: against such there is no law.* **Galatians 5:22-23**

In verse 3 we understand that those who walk in the Spirit or possess the Spirit of God digest the fruit of the Spirit which consists of love, joy, peace, longsuffering, gentleness, goodness, faith, meekness and temperance. In verse 2 we understand that only the righteous can produce true acts of righteousness and they possess the fruit of the Spirit. Lastly, from what we have gathered from verses 2 and 3, verse 1 is interpreted as saying, that the fruit of the righteous is the fruit of the Spirit therefore, the fruit of the righteous is a Tree of Life. In conclusion, if we the righteous consume the fruit of the Spirit we should produce a Tree of Life.

So I ask you, where is The Tree of Life and where are its seeds? If you answered that we are the seeds of The Tree of Life that's in heaven and we produce a Tree of Life every time we exhibit the fruit of the Spirit on earth, you would be correct. We are righteous men walking in the Kingdom of God on earth, producing the fruit of the Spirit which comes from The Tree of Life.

SIDE BAR: Ezekiel 31 speaks of a cedar tree having fair branches. The waters made this tree great. The deep set the tree up on high because of the rivers running round. Therefore the height of the tree was exalted above all other types...and the tree's branches became long because of the multitude of waters. All the fowls of heaven made their nests in this tree's boughs, and under its branches did all the beasts of the field bring forth their young, and under this tree's shadow dwelt all great nations." Are you a tree of life?

Are you that Kingdom walker? Are you producing a Tree of Life? Are you producing the fruit of the Spirit, offering others a chance to taste the fruit of the Tree of Life? Do you walk about the Kingdom with up lifted arms of praise giving applauds and approval of the glory of God? Does your praise pull harsh emissions from the atmosphere filtering and ridding it of pride, the sickness of envy and the stench of greed, by esteeming others higher? Do you have the capacity to absorb the excess former and latter rains when the times of refreshing comes? Are you beautiful to be admired bringing value to the real estate of the Kingdom? Does your praise create a home for the Living God? Does your praise allow you to do something as insignificant as cleaning the bathroom and as important as delivering the Life given Word of God, that will keep its dwellers alive?

Let's look at another tree in the Garden called the Tree of the Knowledge of Good and Evil. It is from this tree we inherit the term **"forbidden fruit"** which is a metaphor describing any object of desire whose appeal also accompanies the knowledge that the object should not be obtained. Forbidden can also describe someone or even thoughts that may be wanted but should not be acquired or entertained.

This tree stood along with the many other beautiful trees that God made and was located in the middle of the <u>Garden of Eden</u> <u>Genesis 2:9</u> having real fruit from which <u>God</u> directly forbade <u>Adam</u> to eat. *"And the LORD God commanded the man, saying, Of every tree of the garden thou mayest freely eat: But of the tree of the knowledge of good and evil, thou shalt not eat of it: for in the day that thou eatest thereof thou shalt surely die."* <u>Genesis 2:17</u> Adam and Eve had no experience with conscience but lived in the innocence or ignorance of knowing right and wrong. Most definitions define conscience with having an awareness of right and wrong, but it also alludes to having your own inner thoughts. Their body and spirit was fused as one by the inner soul that was in harmonic fellowship with God, therefore, Adam and Eve along with their mind, will and emotions were in singular fellowship with God, His purpose and the destiny He had for their lives.

This tree is sometimes called the Tree of Conscience, for the day that you eat of this tree *"you will be as gods knowing good and evil."* Genesis 3:5

Eve, who was aware of the prohibition, ate of the <u>forbidden fruit</u> from the Tree of Knowledge of Good and Evil and gave to her husband that was with her. <u>Genesis 3:1-6</u> For the Bible says, that *"when the woman saw that the tree was good for food, and that it was pleasant to the eyes, and a tree to be desired to make one wise, she took of the fruit thereof, and did eat, and gave also unto her husband with her; and he did eat...the eyes of them both were opened, and they knew that they were naked.* Genesis 3:6

Naturally, they both had physical eyes that saw all the animals for naming and spiritual eyes to understand the things of the Spirit of God. Remembering that man is triune, body soul and spirit, the only eyes that could possibly be opened at this point, were the eyes of their soul. Adam, before eating of the forbidden fruit was never lead by his own conscience as he was all filled with the Spirit of God and His will only.

Unfortunately, Adam was given the responsibility and he willed against the will of God and today every man born after the first man is a creature of Free will against the will of God. That is why you must be born again, willing to seek, receive and execute the will of God and not your own.

As a result of their decision to eat the forbidden fruit, Adam and Eve lost their <u>innocence,</u> became aware of their nakedness <u>Genesis 3:6-7</u> and were immediately exiled from the garden. They were forced to survive through the noble occupation of <u>agriculture</u> *"by the sweat of their brow"* <u>Genesis 3:19-24</u>

The Tree of the Knowledge of Good and Evil was the tree of decision for Adam and Eve. Adam made his choice, what is your tree of decision? What decision is before you that will kick you out or keep you out? What choices are keeping you out of the Kingdom where God is the King? What people are keeping you out of His fellowship? What situations are keeping you out of His will?

Choose you this day (for the rest of your life) *whom ye will serve...* Joshua 24:15 <u>2 Peter 3:9</u> is quoted, *"The Lord is not slack concerning His promise, as some men count slackness; but is longsuffering to us-ward, not willing that any should perish, but that all should come to repentance."* God is not slack in His promises but He desires man to choose repentance, obedience and eternal life. It is not the will of God that any should perish, but He pleas and is longsuffering toward man.

If man was not able to choose, why would God place two trees in the midst of the Garden and say "choose!" <u>Deuteronomy 30:19</u> says, *"I have set before you life and death, blessing and cursing: therefore choose life that both thou and thy seed may live."* Choose life, choose light, choose to obey the Lord, choose to work in His Kingdom, choose to expand His Kingdom, choose to guard the Kingdom way of life, choose to guard your thinking and choose to seek knowledge from God.

It is not for me to debate the issues of your beliefs, Free will or predestination, but it is my desire to admonish you to gather your faith, all your soul, mind and strength and choose Christ. Jesus said, *"I am the **way**, the **truth**, and the **life**: no man cometh unto the Father, but by me." John 14:6*

The purpose of the Tree of the Knowledge of Good and Evil was to reveal the loyalty and heart of man. Does it still exist, who can know? But of a truth, where the Bible stops, we stop. There has never been another mention of this tree again, not from Adam and Eve nor has it been mentioned through scriptures. This tree may or may not be in existence, but the decision still remains, who will you serve?

One thing seems to have remained, the fruit and the seeds of the tree. The fruit of this tree can be seen in every person born in sin and shaped in iniquity as a result of Adam's sin. Its seeds can be seen today in man's ever increasing thirst for worldly knowledge and not God. Daniel 12:4 says, *"even to the time of the end: many shall run to and fro, and knowledge shall be increased."*

God has given man a chance, even a second chance to choose. Many have come to know Him as the God of a second change. Our God is a God of mercy. He has set a precedent in heaven! When lucifer and his angels rebelled in heaven, He casted them out. When Adam and Eve committed the act of sin, He sent them forth from the Garden of Eden. When you or I however, Kingdom dwellers, commit an act against the Father, He shows us mercy! And not just once but over and over again. Could this be the reason the scriptures ask: *"What is man, that thou art mindful of him? and the Son of man, that thou visitest him? For thou hast made him a little lower than the angels, and hast crowned him with glory and honor."* Psalms 8:4.5 When this passage is read, it seems to come from someone who has clearly seen God's M O, "modus operandi" Latin for method of operation. The method of operation was this; you sin you get casted out. So they would ask, *"These made lower than the angels....why are these given another chance, they too have sinned!!! And then to add insult*

to injury not only were they not casted out but You visit them!!!"
WOW.

It is still the duty of man to have dominion, to be fruitful, multiply, replenish the earth and subdue it. Genesis 1:26-28   But what is more important is our ability to choose. The question is still raised; will you serve God or man? Choose life today, keep the mind-set of the Kingdom, obey God's law and stay within the borders of the Kingdom of God.

Chapter VI
Industrial Revolution

After Adam's fall and expulsion from the Garden, they were forced to live with the memories of their former home. They were still expected to have dominion, replenish and subdue, but somehow things were quite different. It remained in them the desire, talents and skills to produce the same byproduct of their previous labor, while the conditions were different.

Due to the sin of Adam God pronounced, *"Cursed is the ground for thy sake; in sorrow shalt thou eat of it all the days of thy life; thorns also and thistles shall it bring forth to thee; and thou shalt eat the herb of the field; in the sweat of thy face shalt thou eat bread"...* Genesis 3:17-19 They now had to work with an unyielding earth, in changing atmospheric surroundings and live in a place where the presence of God was not just the same.

It's amazing how the scriptures say nothing about the expulsion of animals but we can imagine that one by one their nature and character changed also. But chapters 11 & 65 in the Book of Isaiah informs us that there will come a day like the days of the beginning, when the wolf and the lamb shall feed together, the lion shall eat straw like the bullock, the leopard shall lie down with the kid, the cow and the bear shall feed and their young ones shall lie down together: and the lion shall eat straw like the ox and a little child shall lead them.

The Eden or Kingdom experience since being destroyed or put away, can only exist now in the minds of men, hence the phrase "Kingdom minded." In Luke 17:21 Jesus said, *"The Kingdom of God is within you."*

Before the reign of Adam in the Garden, it is very interesting when we notice in the scripture during creation as it describes the light, moon, sun, etc. were for signs and seasons but they were not factors for consideration. We also notice that there was no mention of signs in heaven or changing seasons during the occupation of Adam and Eve in the Garden of Eden, as the mist or dew of the earth watered the grounds, having no involvement or movement from above. There were no signs on the earth or seasonal changes based on the fact that Adam and Eve were never clothed with anything other than the covering of God and nothing else for their natural flesh.

It is only seen at the disturbance of the Kingdom and the cursing of the ground and earth that the scriptures begin to reveal changes on the earth's surface and in the firmament. *"All the fountains of the great deep were broken up, and the windows of heaven were opened and the rain fell upon the earth forty days and forty nights during the time of Noah."* Genesis 7:11, 12

Man had to figure out a way to experience in obedience, the Kingdom of God where God rules. He had to keep his relationship with the King against the constant assaults and influences from the prince of this world. Needless to say, that in the years that followed man shifted his mind-set from the Kingdom of God to that of the kingdoms of this world. Man's focus shifted to work the land/world that would produce prestige, power and wealth for himself. Keeping the balance within the animal kingdom, keeping the balance within the family for stability for generations to come and for keeping proper balance of fellowship with God was no longer his priority. He still has the power to work it, grow it and keep it but it was all for himself.

We find many of the early civilizations beginning revolutions along major river systems. For example the Egyptians settled along the Nile River, the Chinese Empire along the Huang River and the Mesopotamian Countries along the Tigris and Euphrates rivers. In the 1700's the agriculture revolution started taking place which led to a large increase in the production of crops. The Industrial Revolution that affected every aspect of human life was a period of time where there were gigantic shifts in the areas of agriculture, manufacturing, coal mining and transportation. The word revolution denotes an abrupt and rapid change from the manner in which things were once being done. This rush resulted in an increase in food, technology, techniques and profits. The field of agriculture was the leading cause that moved manpower to animal power, and animal power to machine, all of which increased production rates and profits. To show the rapid movement of the Industrial Revolution, let's consider the single invention of the cotton gin.

Cotton, considered a viable source of raw material of the industry played an important role in the Industrial Revolution. Eli Whitney who attended the Yale College in 1789 and at the age of 23 he invented the cotton gin. During those days farming cotton required hundreds of man-hours to separate the small cottonseed from the raw cotton fibers. Eli Whitney's invention removed the cottonseed and could generate up to fifty pounds of cleaned cotton daily. This invention quickly made cotton production profitable for the southern states that produced it. The Northern states profited quickly as well, as they purchased the cotton to produce clothing. Many of the southern states began switching their crops to cotton only not rotating their crops as properly prescribe and then increased slavery for profit. The northern states wanted the cotton but they were against slavery. Many other tensions arose between the southern and northern states, hence in short, the Civil War.

New implements of Industrial Revolution were seen as the knowledge of agriculture grew, for example: by combining crop rotation, manure and better soil preparation this would lead to a steady increase of crop. The invention of steam power and later gas powered engines brought a whole new dimension to the production of crops. The building of large factories, farming machinery and power plants brought men, women and families out of the country and into the cities. In many areas around the factories and plants anywhere from 1 to 4 people lived in single-room dwellings, with many more occupying just two rooms. In the late 1900's overcrowding was five times worse and growing. Conditions were poor with little sanitation and the spread of infectious disease spread rapidly. Fever, cholera and other epidemics killed thousands and the death rate was doubled among children under five. Many cities were considered lethal places to live in due to the mortality rates of nearly sixty-percent of that in the rural areas.

As the desire for automobiles, airplanes and the railroad increased many more power plants were built. As the increase of technology with its appliances relied on electricity, the need for this natural resource increased proportionately. The production of electricity was and is still generated by the use of coal & oil-fired power plants.

Unlike the French Revolution, this Industrial Revolution will never end. As the knowledge of man steadily increases during these last and evil days, there will be steady increases in his inventions, desires, discoveries and imaginations.

Yet, with all the technological inventions, witty inventions and huge breakthroughs in the midst of this changing revolution, as recent as 100 years ago, the record indicates that, at least four-fifths of the world's population is still in some way dependant on agriculture. It has also been suggested that half of the worlds working population is employed in the field of agriculture.

When we consider the Industrial Revolution of the Kingdom of God, we must firstly agree that the time and atmosphere we are living in today is not the same as in the times of our forefathers, grandmothers or even from the memories of our childhood. We must go back to the times when God was first, the man was the head and priest of the family and the way of survival was an inheritance passed down from generation to generation. "We must go back to the times when the praises were pure and the hallelujahs were holy." *Bishop Joseph N. Williams*

Let's go way back to the time when Adam and Eve, *"...heard the voice of the LORD God walking in the garden in the cool of the day."* Genesis 3:8 Let's go way back to a perfect place where man experienced the assembling of themselves together with God, knowing that when two or three gather together, that God was in the midst. Let's go back to the place where man was in continued fellowship and dialogue with God which was their prayer life. In the beginning, man experienced fellowship, relationship and had a prayer life, but after the fall of man, the expulsion from Eden and the curse upon the earth, Genesis 4:26 says, *"Then began men to call upon the name of the LORD."* If they had just been obedient there would have been no need for sacrifice. *"...Behold, to obey is better than sacrifice, and to hearken than the fat of rams."* 1 Samuel 15:22 What Samuel would have said to Adam in this instance would have been something like, *"If you had obeyed God there would be no need for the sacrifice. You should have listened to and obeyed the voice of the Lord rather than the voice of your fleshly desires."*

Because of man's disobedience, the earth and they that dwell therein are experiencing their own industrial revolution and not God's revolution. God's revolution would have come about with the spoken Word of the **Father**, the creativity and ingenuity of the **Son** and by the movement over the face of the earth by the **Spirit**.

The word **industry** is a broad term that can be used to describe any kind of economic production that uses raw materials. The word industry comes from Latin roots and is defined as the manufacturing of a good (product) or service within a certain category. God has given and has endowed His citizens with their own form of occupation that produces goods and provides services vital to the Kingdom of God. We are able to produce the product of His character, the raw products of His fruits and the services His gifts affords. The word **revolution** comes from the Latin word *revolutio* which means a turn around, a change in power or the way things are done within a relatively short period of time. Revolutions of every kind come for the sole purpose of change. But the revolution that God's brings makes life more abundant, comfortable and prosperous for its occupants. Revolutions have been noted in every facet of life, but listed below are a few examples of the various revolutions that have taken place in the Kingdom of God.

There have been revolutions in the areas of:

Our Work ethics-In the early days of ministry people viewed their service to the Kingdom very differently than they do now. Work ethics encompass a set of values based on the belief that if you take the initiative to work hard it will bring benefits and enhance character. The saints of God believed in serving the poor, aiding the widow, comforting the sick and embracing the orphans. Even with the lack of skills, education and strategies the service of preaching, evangelism, culinary arts, administration, missions, and soul winning were the primary focus of ministry. They were considered reasonable services and rendered without charge. The level of dedication to prayer, having a prayer life and corporate times of prayer were deemed one of the greatest of these works, for prayer is work. These acts of service have paved the way and have revolutionized the Kingdom with the advancement of technology of media. The work of God has advanced through televised services of healings, deliverances, Bible teachings and conferences. Our increase in the wisdom of financial strategies, have enabled the purchase of major properties, buildings, churches, schools and auditoriums. These properties of Kingdom ownership enable expansion and advancements within the Kingdom preparing in excellence, for the many souls coming into glory.

<u>Our Giftings</u>-The use of gifts was always a sign of the movement and the power of God. Gifts from God come without repentance, but there was a time when they were considered sacred, displayed with fear and received with reverence. Through religious and secular education and mentoring, the evolving and increase of giftings have become more effective as their intent, their order and its placement are now better understood. This paves the way for others that God has endowed with similar gifts and calls to minister to the unchurched by the power of God and bring perfection to the body of Christ.

<u>Women in ministry</u>-In scripture women were not always visible nor were they allowed a voice as was customary in days gone by. As it was foretold by the prophet Joel of the Spirit of God, *"It shall come to pass afterward, that I will pour out my spirit upon all flesh; and your sons and your daughters shall prophesy, your old men shall dream dreams, your young men shall see visions."* Joel 2:28 Women in ministry in the beginning was slow moving, however the body of Christ have come to realize that women are called, have value and function within the Kingdom of God. Women not only have the ability to nurture but they have become elders, pastors, prayer warriors, prophets, televangelist, etc. They encounter many souls through media, entertainment, conferences, books and seminars. Having "Women in ministry" is prevalent in the areas of influence, as women outnumber men in the Kingdom of God.

These revolutions and many more have helped to shape the Kingdom into what we see and have experienced today. What is the category of your industry? How are you adding to the Kingdom's revolution? What is your product? Is it good? Have you perfected it? What services can you bring to the table? How does it impact your family, co-laborers, neighborhood, state or nation? If you have not tapped into your industry it would be in your best interest to spend some time in prayer. When the Lord returns, you don't want to be labeled as an unprofitable servant. Matthew 25

To aid in the discovery or confirmation of your industry, inquire about the newly released workbook "Kingdom Industrial Revolution" I know my Industry by Dr. S. Kelly.

Chapter VII
Pollution

Pollution! Pollution! What is it? Pollution is any substance that is in the atmosphere, considered poisonous. Pollution is when our air, land and water contain harmful substances. Chemicals, toxic fumes and wastes byproducts that have been deposited and are harming humans, wildlife, plant life, our land, sea and air are considered pollutants. There are approximately 100,000 man-made synthetic chemicals that are now on the market, with another one thousand new chemicals that are being added to the atmosphere ever year and that is coupled with natural human waste. In America the states of Chicago, St. Louis, Los Angeles and Pittsburg have the hugest intensity and output in industry. We have proof and documentation that the levels of pollution in these areas are the highest and rising.

During the summer vacation my parents would pack the family in the car and we would travel south to visit my grandparents. Of course the way of the south is very different from us northerners. There were three distinctive things that I remember when we would visit. Anytime we were sitting on the porch, the saints, a neighbor or for that matter anyone passing by would drive by and honk their horns. As they were driving by we would wave and as soon as they passed by, we would ask, "Who was that?" Secondly, we raked all the leftover food and bones or what we called scrap food, from our plates into a large bin that was in the back of the house, for the pigs. Lastly, three times a week they would burn the trash in the backyard as a common method to dispose of garbage. Backyard burning of trash in a barrel or piles releases smoke into the air. The smell and the emission of smoke depends on the trash that went into the fire, the temperature of the fire and the available oxygen. Trash containing plastics, polystyrene (such as foam cups), CCA pressure-treated wood and bleached or colored papers can produce harmful chemicals left in the ashes or in the air such as arsenic from treated wood when burned. Passed in 1969, the burning of trash was made illegal in every state however the penalties connected may vary from state to state.

Remember the icon Woodsy Owl? Back in the 70's they drilled in our heads the famous motto, **"Give a hoot — don't pollute!"** and then latter he came out with **"Lend a hand — care for the land!"** Although no one is singing about it now, pollution is still very harmful.

Every chemical we use and every substance we produce in manufacturing or farming remains here on earth. Just because we have disposed of waste down the toilet, burn it or bury it, it's still here on the earth! Waste can only be hidden in several places or changed into another form. When the southern states would burn their garbage in the backyard, you would think that it was incinerated and that was all to it, but as nature would have it the byproducts were only transferred into the atmosphere and held in the clouds waiting to be released on top of your heads, clothing and cars in the form of acid rain.

The World Health Organization reports that 3 million people have died from the effects of air pollution. This is three times the 1 million who die each year from automobile accidents and equivalent to the deaths from breast cancer and prostate cancers combined!

Pollution sources are classified as either point source or nonpoint source (NPS). Point source pollution comes specifically from industrial and sewage treatment plants. Non-Point source pollution occurs when rainfall or snow melt moving over and through the ground, picks up natural and man-made pollutants and finally deposits them into lakes, rivers, wetlands, coastal waters, and even our underground sources of drinking water. These non-point sources may include particles of pollution of fertilizers, herbicides, and insecticides from agricultural lands and residential areas, oil, grease, toxic chemicals and heavy metals from urban runoff and energy production, sediment from improperly managed construction sites, acid drainage from abandoned mines, bacteria from livestock, pet wastes, septic systems and recreational boating to name only a few!

Less than 20 years ago, testing was done on high-doses of man-made chemicals that were released in the atmosphere. It was determined and the evidence is still solid, that these synthetic chemicals have contributed to the dwindling wildlife populations by disrupting their hormones, altering sexual development, impairing reproduction, and undermining their immune system. Any of these man-made chemicals that have been identified from the atmosphere are now called endocrine disruptors. They are called this because they interfere with the body's hormones. The human Endocrine system controls the bodies growth, organ development, metabolism and regular body processes such as kidney function, body temperature and calcium regulation. Endocrine disruptors are the chemicals that interfere with hormones such as thyroid, cortisol, insulin or growth regulators. These chemicals are now being tested for potential links to prostate, testicular and breast cancers, as well as lowered sperm counts, behavioral and learning abnormalities.

The increase in power plants of coal & oil-fired power plants produced pollution equivalent to putting an additional 570,487 cars on the road. It also produces approximately two times the amount of carbon dioxide that is harmful to the atmosphere. The emissions from automobiles produce the most air polluting act an average citizen can contribute. Pollution from coal-fired power plants was allowed to continue because it was cheaper to operate than the gas powered plants. This condition is more than likely to worsen as many of these plants were deregulated because of the *1959 Clean Air Act* passed that grandfathered in the use of many of the older plants that had been constructed. Utilities use these plants, which are allowed to produce up to 10 times more pollution than the newer facilities. The pollution in the air from these old power plants alone contributes to the estimated 30,000 premature deaths, the hundreds of thousands of asthma attacks, and the many thousands of patients that are hospitalized for upper respiratory and cardiovascular illnesses each year.

Can Kingdom dwellers produce pollution in the Kingdom of God by the things that they do? Is the Kingdom atmosphere affected by how the people of God are living? Are toxins being released into the Kingdom of God by the byproducts or second hand smoke of questionable Christian behavior? "Are you toxic or redemptive?" (*Bishop Joseph N. Williams*) If there are actions or an exercise that believers can release into the atmosphere to create a place of response and a place of inhabitation for God, could it also be safe to say that He does not inhabit places considered polluted? If the believer's byproduct of praise is an inhabitation or atmosphere for God here on the earth then the byproduct of many lukewarm Christians would produce barriers of pollution that would block the presence of God. With that said, it is safe to say that there is a type of pollution infiltrating the Kingdom of God. When His people are not producing pure praise, pure worship (lifestyle) and the proper use of their God given giftings they are most likely emitting poisonous byproducts that restrict the movements of the Spirit and are harmful to all that dwell therein.

The scripture conveys that the place of pollution found in the Kingdom of God, is in the hearts of man. The believer is admonished with all their power to be careful about the gateway of the heart, for it is the hidden mind of men. The Bible declares to, *"Keep thy heart with all diligence; for out of it are the issues of life."* Proverbs 4:23 It is the responsibility of the believer to abstain from *pollutants* such as idolatry and fornication Acts 15:20 especially after escaping the pollution of this world through the knowledge of the Lord and Savior Jesus Christ. If the believer is *"again entangled therein, and overcome (by the world's pollution) the latter end is worse with them than the beginning."* 2 Peter 2:20

The seat of man's emotions, live in the mind. These emotions can be triggered by the gateways of the human five senses. The five senses of man are the eye for seeing, the nose for smelling, the tongue for tasting, the touch for touching and the ear for hearing. It is through these gateways that the mind of the believer can be polluted.

Eyes: Just realize the filth that comes from television, movies, books, magazines, classrooms, work areas, pictures, texting messaging, sexting, etc.

Ears: Just think of the grimy sounds that come from the television, radio, movies, school, bosses, cell phone conversations, music, videos, from the car next to yours, from people that speak filthy language, etc.

Tongue: Just think of the filthy communication that you allowed out of your mouth, or the disgusting things that have come in contact with it that were not wholesome to your body or the Spirit of God: drugs, alcohol, body parts, food in excess, and food knowingly against the body, etc.

Touch: Just think of the many repulsive things that have been touched that were filthy and against the Spirit of God: Weapons, another person that was not yours, the touching of yourself, a child or teenager, etc.

Nose: Just think of the putrid smells that trigger gluttony, the lust for the person associated with that perfume or cologne, etc.

These various portals are the means of communication that can enter the mind and produce the smoke, the soot, the smog, the film and ultimately the pollution found in the firmament of the Kingdom of God. These harmful byproducts of the heart manifest themselves as rioting, drunkenness, wantonness, strife, envying, adultery, false witness Romans 13 debates, backbiting, whisperings, 2 Corinthians 12 evil thoughts, fornications, murders, theft, covetousness, wickedness, deceit, lasciviousness, an evil eye, blasphemy, pride, foolishness, uncleanness, lasciviousness, idolatry, witchcraft, hatred, variance, emulations, wrath, seditions, heresies and such alike. Galatians 5

Can you imagine the presence of God trying to weave His way though this thick combination of poisonous fog? Is this the place where His people live and is He to dwell among His people?

With all the changes, revolutions and so called improvements that have taken place in the Kingdom of God, let's consider them and their effects. Revolution has been seen in the pulpits, the music industry, Christian entertainment, church growth, church services, evangelism and exercised giftings just to name a few. Revolutions have been seen in:

Our services: Tarry services, Song services, Testimony services, Deliverance services, Praise and Worship services, etc.

Our music ministry: Song services, Choirs, Caravans, Quartets, Groups, Bands, Record deals, CD contracts, Music videos, etc.

Our meeting places: By the river, in homes, in school houses, churches, Cathedrals, Mega Churches, 1 church in several locations, stadiums, etc.

Our ministry gifts: Brother, Deacons, Minister, Evangelist, Prophet, Prophetess, Pastor, Bishop, Arch Bishop, Apostle, Prelate, etc.

Our Prayer services: Family prayer, All night prayer, Week day prayer, noon-day prayer, house to house prayer, prayer teams, Prayer leaders, Intercessors, Prophetic Intercessors, etc.

Our Evangelism/telemarketing: Word of mouth, pony express, mailing, tent revivals, radio, television, satellite, cable network, live streaming, etc.

Our Bible knowledge: Family study, Sunday School, Bible study, Christian Education, Bible Schools: Bachelors, Masters and Doctorial, School of Prophets, and on line studies, etc.

With all the improvements you would think that our atmosphere would be filled with all the fruit and the gifts of the Spirit. Can you imagine a Kingdom atmosphere filled with all the fruit and the gifts of the Spirit? Can you imagine experiencing a pure and clean atmosphere everywhere you walked, in the people that you met and in every breath that you took? However, it seems that pollutants are being emitted more than that of the Spirit of God.

SIDE BAR: The two main areas of pollution output come from pulpits and from between the pews.

The major problem of any existing pollution is that it not only affects the present areas exerting its effect on all those presently around, but it can also dictate the possibilities of the future, eternity and a person's end. Kingdom citizens may never know the enormous effects, respiratory problems or allergies encountered that one prayer pill simply may be of little effect or will not cure. Many citizens are not aware that their actions are in fact a response to the pressures of the invisible external and internal pollution surrounding the Kingdom.

If every saint would join in the campaign to "Give a hoot" and stop the pollution from within, the clean-up of greed, selfishness, low-self esteem, murder, backbiting, filthy lucre, pride, covetousness and such the like, **can begin!**

The problem of Kingdom pollution is not new as it is seen in Old Testament times. Jeremiah 2:22 says, *"For though thou wash...and take thee much soap, yet thine iniquity is marked before me, saith the Lord GOD. How canst thou say, I am not polluted, I have not gone after Baal?"* Ezekiel 14:11 declares, *"That the house of Israel may go no more astray from me, neither be polluted any more with all their transgressions; but that they may be my people, and I may be their God."* The Lord wants His people pure, true to Him and unpolluted.

Every Christian should desire natural clean air, land and water. But far more important than these elements is the desire to annihilate the pollution that infests the soul, the mind and eventually the body of Kingdom dwellers. Romans 12:2 says, *"And be not conformed (or polluted) to this world: but be ye transformed by the renewing of your mind"* Every believer must be in agreement with God by having a single mind, heart and will synonymous with Him. The separation of man's will is what got Adam and Eve banished from the Garden of Eden. It was the separation of Cain's will that caused the rejection of his offering and fueled the release of jealousy into the atmosphere. This release of jealousy coupled with pride, selfishness and rebellion caused him to kill his own brother which in turn caused another release into the atmosphere, the cry of murder! WOW!!!   Genesis 4:10

It is the separation of the believer's will from God's will that causes the release of pollution into the atmosphere of the Kingdom. The proper alignment of the Kingdom mind-set believer diminishes pollution. Get your mind back! Steve Harvey has a quote that he says almost every morning on his radio show, "Get your mind right!"

The exclusive way that this clean-up campaign can happen is by the renewing and the washing of the minds of the believer. Spiritual renewal of the heart and mind will not come from a 7 step program, a 30 day patch or a one day seminar. Only God has the power to renew minds and to wash hearts. Ephesians 4:22-24 says, *"Put off concerning the former conversation the old man, which is corrupt according to the deceitful lusts; and be renewed in the spirit of your mind; and that ye put on the new man, which after God is created in righteousness and true holiness."* God wants to sanctify and cleanse His church with the washing of water by the Word *"that He might present it to Himself a glorious church, not having spot, or wrinkle, or any such thing; but that it should be holy and without blemish."* Ephesians 5:25-27

In total agreement with the Apostle James, the half brother of Jesus Christ and the author of the book that bears his name, to the saints he writes how to become or remain unpolluted and single with the mind of God. In James 4 he admonished the saints to, *"Submit yourselves therefore to God. Resist the devil, and he will flee from you. Draw nigh to God, and He will draw nigh to you. Cleanse your hands, ye sinners; and purify your hearts, ye double minded. Be afflicted, and mourn, and weep: let your laughter be turned to mourning, and your joy to heaviness. Humble yourselves in the sight of the Lord, and He shall lift you up. Speak not evil one of another."*

Cleansing of the atmosphere takes place when the believer obeys the commands of Jesus Christ. Jesus put it very simply when He said, *"He that believeth (have the same mind) and is baptized (washed from the pollutions of this world) shall be saved."* Mark 16:16 The believer is still in the world but the pollution and filth of the world is no longer in him. John 17:11, 16; Philippians 2:15 When the enemy comes, he should find none (pollutants) in us.

It is also very important that the citizens of the Kingdom realize that when the mind becomes infiltrated with the pollutions of the world, that it affects their proper response to the will and desire of the Spirit of God. For example, when the true Word of God is preached or when it is studied, God's Word is not appealing or of little effect to the infected hearer. Just as poison in the stomach will cause good food to regurgitate, the believer regurgitates the Word of God every time they are hearers only and not doers of the Word. The believer needs the Word of God. No matter how hard it may be, the more you take it in the easier it will go down. Receiving the cleansing blood of Jesus Christ and the washing of the Word of God is the only way to bring forgiveness and cleansing to the soul.

Let's come to the conclusion regarding pollution manifested in the Kingdom of God. Pollution is on the rise. Pollution is produced when the will of God is not obeyed. Pollution is also produced when the byproducts of what we so call doing His will in fact really excretes the hidden, wrong motives and improper attitudes either individually or corporately. God speaks very plainly in scripture against pollution of the soul but He makes a way of escape!

God in the book of Revelation speaks very plainly against the lukewarm Christian. Lukewarm Christians are individuals that produce less emissions, but pollution nevertheless. These Christians are compared to other energy sources that are capable of producing powering but create less pollution unlike today's gasoline having the highest emissions of released pollutants. These power producers that create less pollution include alcohols, electricity, natural gas, and propane. They are called "clean fuels." Many Christians believe they are clean but when you check their emissions they are really like those so called clean fuels that are not really clean at all!!! The Bible says that a *"little leaven leaveneth the whole lump."* Galatians 5:9. Man attempts to compromise or slow down the Greenhouse effect by creating what they call hybrids, which again emits the so called "clean pollution." But God says, *"I know thy works, that thou art neither cold nor hot... but lukewarm, and neither cold nor hot, I will spue thee out of my mouth."* Revelation 3:15-16

The living God is able to save and cleanse every polluted person and the pollution that they create. The Spirit of God is able to take the unregenerate soul out of his filthy environment and translate him into the Kingdom of Light. You can escape the pollutions of this world through the knowledge of the Lord and Savior Jesus Christ. You can experience purification by obeying the Word of Truth. Colossians 1:13; 2 Peter 2:20 To the Kingdom dwellers, to the co-labors of the Gospel and those that have been translated from darkness into the Light, don't become the Kingdom's garbage collectors or incinerators! Be careful of your emissions because "everything you produce will find a use!" Remember! "Spirits are transferable." Pollution that is produced is not simply disposed of. It will either become a harmful invisible blockage of the move of God, it will either be transformed, or it will be transfer to someone else. What is most dangerous about pollution is that it can remain hidden waiting for the most inopportune time in your life to manifest. God's wants you to be a part of His revolution; you are the product producing the goods without the byproducts of pollutants. You are necessary in the scheme and arrangement of the Kingdom.

Automobiles and power plants have to go through the rigorous testing of emissions inspection, why not Kingdom dwellers? It's time for every believer to pass inspection! To pass you must have faith in God, repent, be obedient and a doer of the Word of God. Do it today. Let Him in to your hearts today.

Repeat this short prayer.

FATHER AND CREATOR, YOU MADE ME AND YOU KNOW ALL ABOUT ME. I HAVE SINNED AGAINST YOU AND NEED YOUR FORGIVENESS. YOU DESIRE ONLY TRUTH AND WISDOM IN MY INWARD PARTS. SO PURGE ME, DEAR LORD, AND TAKE OUT EVERYTHING THAT'S NOT LIKE YOU OR EXHORTS ITSELF AGAIN THE KNOWLEDGE OF WHO YOU ARE AND I SHALL BE CLEAN. WASH ME WITH YOUR WORD AND I SHALL BE WHITER THAN SNOW. MAKE ME THE TREE OF LIFE PLANTED BY THE RIVERS OF WATER, UNMOVABLE, IMPARTING TRUTH AND RELEASING THE KNOWLEDGE OF ETERNAL LIFE TO ALL WHO COME IN CONTACT. AMEN.

The Apostle Peter is quoted, *"Seeing ye have purified your souls in your obedience to the truth, unto unfeigned love of the brethren..."* you are born again through the Word of God, which liveth and abideth forever." 1 Peter 1:22, 23

Chapter VIII
The Green House Effect

Planets have been discovered over the years in our galaxy but none of them have been determined safe for human inhabitation. Earth is the only planet capable of hosting the proper air composition and temperature necessary to support human, animal and plant life. The sun is earth's primary energy source, sending light, heat and other rays through the atmosphere needed for life. Plant life gives off oxygen (O2) and takes carbon dioxide (C02) from the air, recycling the atmosphere, keeping it fresh. The heated earth keeps the atmosphere bearable and adds moister to the air from water sources.

The greenhouse effect is a natural exchange that occurs between the sun and the earth. The sun beams down rays heating up the earth and the stratosphere (firmament) that captures the heat, keeping the atmosphere and surface of the Earth warm enough to sustain human life. Without the greenhouse effect the planet would be uninhabitable, a frozen wasteland.

To describe the Greenhouse effect taking place on the earth we can look at the glass houses that are purposely constructed to create this same effect. Greenhouses are usually made using glass walls and glass roofing. Within this controlled environment, this building serves to house and grow plants, flowers and small trees for cultivation and exhibition. The Greenhouse effect happens when the sun rays, namely infrareds, enter through the glass walls and roof. These rays are then absorbed and released as heat within and are now trapped inside heating the entire area. These heat levels must be monitored. If the temperature inside the greenhouse gets too hot, plants will wither and die. Possibly developing a daily routine that maintain the optimum temperature or having an escape hatch for heat release may be something to consider. Remember, it may take one hot hour to destroy everything in the greenhouse.

Many drivers have experienced the same greenhouse phenomena inside of their cars. Some of the heat from the sun is absorbed by the seats, the dashboard and the carpeting. These objects then release the heat but it doesn't all go back through the windows. Some of the heat is reflected back inside making the inside nice, toasty and warm, hence the greenhouse effect.

Before the Industrial Revolution, the amount of carbon dioxide (CO_2) and other greenhouse gases released and exchanged into the atmosphere were in balance with Earth. After the Industrial Revolution took off, man began emitting large amounts of pollution that came from the byproducts of cars, trucks, factories, planes and power plants. Also adding to the greenhouse effect is deforesting and over population. As it has been proven over time an extra-thick heating blanket of gaseous pollutants began surrounding the entire Earth.

The heat released from the sun rays along with the heat released from the earth that is trapped within the atmosphere by the blanket of pollution are the elements that have created the greenhouse effect in the firmament on the earth. As time and pollution have prevailed this effect has been established and documented. When the greenhouse effect is established there must be some type of valve or hatch door for heat release. If the conditions in an established greenhouse ever become too hot, the leather seats, the plants and the people will be destroyed. The earth which is now experiencing greenhouse effects can suffer grave damages if the temperature is off by one degree Fahrenheit. Well, research has shown that for over the past century the globe has heated up a little over one degree Fahrenheit.

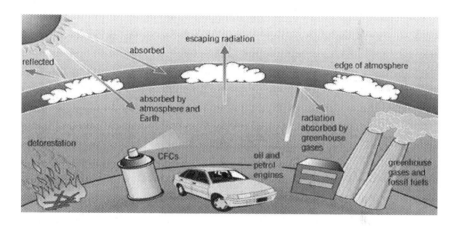

Likewise in the Kingdom of God, He firstly planted everything we need to produce, within. He then watered, pruned and sends the increase. He has sent His rays of exceeding, abundantly and above all that we could ask or think. He has sent His sun that *"rises on the evil and on the good, and rain that falls on the just and on the unjust."* Matthew 5:45 So, what has been produced?

As a unit, Kingdom dwellers have produced and created waves of heat, even smoke as from a sacrifice that goes up to God our Creator in the form of praise, obedience, proper representation, growth, seed after His own kind and many more elements that are pleasing in

His sight, savory to His nose and even sweet sounding in His ears. They have also produced heat waves that came from strange fire and if that was not enough heat, add it to the heat generated by the pollution already created by murders, drunkenness, revellings, and such the like: create heat waves that do nothing but bounce back into the Kingdom atmosphere creating more heat in the atmosphere affecting every citizen.

Where is the escape hatch in the Kingdom of God? Where is the valve? What will deliver the Kingdom from these heat waves of destruction and death? What can stop the withering of souls, the melting of dreams, and the fading of vision?

Only the obedience, purity, true worship, praise, fervent prayer, service to the poor, charity, joy, peace, bowles of mercies, humbleness of mind, longsuffering, gentleness, goodness, faith, meekness, temperance and the love for God by the Kingdom dwellers can save the Kingdom from the effects of a major melt down. More than ever, it will take an abundance of these antidotes to heal the skies of every Kingdom mind from these poisons.

If this continuing trend is not eliminated, will it will lead us to Kingdom Warming?

Chapter IX
Kingdom Warming
Global Warming

Global warming is the term used to describe the actual temperature increase of earth's air, land surface and oceans. There are some that believe that the whole concept of the earth heating up is nothing more than a big hoax. But Global warming has been recorded since the mid 20th century and our earth's temperature has only continued to increase. The major contributor of the elevated temperatures of the skies and the earth is due to the Green House effect. These increases may not seem much in number as the average temperatures climbed an additional 1.4 degrees Fahrenheit around the world since the 1880's. A little over one degree doesn't sound like a substantial amount, but this increase has caused:

- sea levels to raise losing land mass and beaches
- the disappearance of coral reefs-instinction of marine life
- birds to shift further northward before their usual time
- changes in the amount and pattern of precipitation
- increase in the number of forest fires-due to dry seasons
- increase in insect growth and infestation-West Nile & Ticks
- arctic shrinkage of glaciers and mountain snow

- the reduction of agricultural yield-due to frost or drought
- ongoing extinction of species-in the oceans & forests
- changes in the course of human diseases-West Nile, asthma

and the list goes on and on. The planet earth is experiencing universally heated waters, skies and land, hence Global warming.

We have all read about, witnessed and lived through many of the increasing natural disasters that have affected our families, neighborhoods, cities, states, nation and entire world. To name a few: tsunamis, earthquakes, avalanches, floods, volcanic eruptions, hurricanes and tornadoes. The Global warming effect is dreadfully enormous, that is why many man hours of examination, comparison, huge research projects and tons of funding have gone into trying to find out why and how if at all possible to stop its effects.

Taken from the data above let's review two phenomenon's that are currently listed as a direct effect of GW (1) The strange migrations of birds and (2) Deforesting.

1 The strange migrations of birds:

An ecologist observes the behavior of birds. Can their observation of birds migrating up North add to the truth concerning GW? Data collected from NASA, universities and independent studies inform us that the season of spring has been arriving earlier and earlier with each passing year. For many scientists, it's a clean cut pattern and a fact, that many birds are shifting their time of migration as a result of the climate or temperature changes, and yet other birds are not. What's going on? When GW is in effect not only are the migrations sooner but it causes their whole community to get out of synch. The plants that birds eat begin blooming much earlier and the insects that they eat have begun showing up three weeks earlier causing many of the would be or slow migrating birds to mis-time their needed prey for survival. Those that cannot keep up with the constant climate changes have declined in their appearance.

As we compare the robin species that migrate short-distances with the wood thrush that migrate for long-distances, we will see the effects of bird migration and how it differs from species to species. The wood thrush who is slow to change, arrives at his summer location on May 6, which is only one day earlier than normal. The robin however, adapts quickly to his climate change, begins his migration early and reaches his summer location on March 5 instead of the usual March 26, that's 21 days earlier than usual. A new meaning is given to the phrase "the early bird." The robin that is sensitive to the atmospheric changes is the one who starts out early for his northern summer home. He reaches the location days before his usual time. He now has the option to enter into any one of the many previously drilled condominium holes made by woodpeckers. The robin's watchful eye of the skies and it changing seasons keeps him on time to catch the "early worm," the plants and any other insect that maybe experiencing the same effects of the atmosphere. The birds that are slow and are so far off are losing out on what the land can offer, ownership and a place for their families.

2 Deforesting:

Rainforests, forest or just trees, are believed to provide a significant amount of the world's oxygen. Oxygen is produced during the process called photosynthesis. This is when living plants and living trees remove carbon dioxide from the atmosphere and release oxygen during their normal respiration. There are many benefits of having trees on the earth. Here are a few examples of their benefits, they:

- slow down the greenhouse effect
- they add moisture to the air
- they cool the streets and the city
- they conserve energy with their shade
- save water by slowing water evaporation for drying lawns
- prevents water floods or water contamination by behaving like a big sponge during a storm
- mark the seasons
- provide a canopy and habitat for wildlife
- provide wood
- increase property values

Having trees are like the lungs of the earth, that take in CO_2 (carbon dioxide) and exhale O_2 (oxygen).

Deforesting or Deforestation is defined as the clearance of naturally occurring forest. This can be accomplished by logging or by fire. Some of the reasons given for deforesting include the use of land for livestock, agriculture, and real estate. If trees are removed without sufficient reasoning, and are not replaced or reforested, the land and earth is on the path to becoming wasteland. Many developing countries are denied the opportunity to cut down their forests in pursuit of the many monetary benefits that the United States experienced as deforestation is now viewed as detrimental. Deforestation is a major cause of the green house effect and a direct contributor to GW. If the increase of deforestation continues the earth will experience further strange phenomena's lurking in the skies along with it increasing temperatures.

Romans 14:17 says *"the Kingdom of God is not meat and drink; but righteousness, and peace, and joy in the Holy Ghost."* The Kingdom of God is **righteousness**. No one can live right or righteously without the help of the Lord. To have righteousness is to have God present at all times ready to assist our lives. The Holy Spirit, our Helper is called to our side to help us every day of our lives. John 14:16 The Kingdom of God is **peace**. That means we are to live in wholeness, complete, with nothing missing and nothing broken. It is a peace that brings calmness and assurance, even in the midst of a storm. This peace comes by way of accepting the Lord Jesus as Savior, which allows you to have peace with God. Experiencing tranquility based on the relationship with you and Christ will afford you the peace of God. John 14:27 It means being anointed to live and enjoy this life in all of its fullness. John 1:16 The Kingdom of God is **joy**. Far greater than the feeling of happiness that cannot be taken away due to life's curves, is the joy of the Lord. Knowing that He is with you, everything else will be alright. John 15:11 It means having the anointing to live everyday filled with gladness having the supernatural joy of the Lord that comes from within! John 16:24

The Kingdom of God is within us. It has been given to us for our benefit. We can't buy it, sell it or control it. The same Kingdom rule that was given to Adam and Eve, in Eden is also given to you. The Kingdom dwellers are to experience the Kingdom in the place where God reigns and rules. His people are in relationship with Him. They have a mind to obey and to work. They seek to maintain family by working the land together. They still have dominion over the fish, fowl, beast and every creepy thing and responsibility to maintain optimum balance and conditions for the animal kingdom. It is still the charge of man to advance, establish and experience the Kingdom of God. Only those who are Kingdom minded are ready to work it, grow it and keep it, until the whole earth is filled with the harvest of His Glory.

Let us also review the same two phenomena's occurring in the natural world that may be occurring within the Kingdom of God, causing Kingdom Warming: (1) The strange migration of the Kingdom dwellers and (2) Deforesting of Kingdom trees.

1 The strange migration of the Kingdom dwellers:

Migration is the movement of a group of objects, organisms, animals or people and it can be permanent or temporary. Migration has always been a traditional response or method of survival when confronted with change or the aftermath of a tragedy.

As a result of Kingdom dwellers actions and byproducts within the Kingdom of God there has been an alarming increase of devastating disasters. The volcanic eruptions of husbands that beat their wife's, the floods of pregnancies by pastors with their congregants, the avalanches of fallout that occur when the leader passes on and no one has been appointed to continue the work, the off the chart earthquakes that shook the very foundations of the Catholic faith as their priest's were exposed for mishandling the altar boys and the expected aftershocks that rippled throughout the Pentecostal, Protestant and Jehovah's witness' exposing the very same sex crimes and the tsunami that swept away churches that could not pay their rent, leases or mortgages, are all events that are the direct result of Kingdom warming.

SIDE BAR: Going unsaid are nuclear fall-out and terrorism in the pews.

Our Kingdom skies should be filled with the beams from the Light of God. Our skies should manifest a proper balance of the exchange of love, joy, peace and righteousness, from Him to us and from us to Him. But, as truth would have it our Kingdom atmospheric skies are overshadowed and hampered by the pollutions of rioting, drunkenness, wantonness, strife, envying, adultery, false witness Romans 13 debates, backbiting, whisperings, 2 Corinthians 12 evil thoughts, fornications, murders, theft, covetousness, wickedness, deceit, lasciviousness, an evil eye, blasphemy, pride, foolishness, uncleanness, idolatry, witchcraft, hatred, variance, emulations, wrath, seditions, heresies and such alike. Galatians 5

1 Chronicles 12:32 says, *"And of the children of Issachar, which were men that had understanding of the times, to know what...ought to be done."* Likewise the children of God, when seeing these things should know what to do. RUN! LEAVE! MIGRATE! Go North! Because *"fair (wonderful, pleasant) weather cometh out of the north: with God is terrible (huge) majesty."* Job 37: 22 Jesus asked His disciples, *"Can ye not discern the signs of the times?"* Matthew 16:3 Jesus is asking those who claim to be His disciples are you children of Issachar, able to know what ought to be done in these times? Many Kingdom dwellers are finally beginning to recognize the signs of the times. For *"there shall be signs in the sun, and in the moon, and in*

the stars; and upon the earth distress of nations, with perplexity; the sea and the waves roaring; men's hearts failing them for fear, and for looking after those things which are coming on the earth: for the powers of heaven shall be shaken." Luke 2:25, 26 All these signs in the heavens and on the earth all point to the coming of the Lord. It is now the responsibility of every believer to begin to move. Move out of your comfort zones and go to the place or places that God has designed for you. This place does not only contain the need for a closer relationship with Him but it includes His will for your life.

Have you heard? God is speaking into the atmosphere. There is only one atmosphere; it is shared by the kingdom of darkness and the Kingdom of Light. Do you remember reading about the war in heaven between Michael and his angels who were against satan and his angels? They all fought in the same atmosphere. Revelation 12:7 Do you remember when Daniel prayed and his answer was held up? The angel of the Lord said *"Fear not, Daniel: for from the first day that thou didst set thine heart to understand and to chasten thyself before thy God, thy words were heard, and I am come for thy words, but the prince of the kingdom of Persia withstood me one and twenty days: but, lo, Michael, one of the chief princes, came to help me; and I remained there with the kings of Persia. Now I am come to make thee understand."* Daniel 10:12-14 From these passages we come to understand that Light and dark fought in the same atmosphere, the place where God's Words are released!

If you can hear Him, He's speaking to you. He's speaking to the writers to begin writing books, to the songsters to record, to the business owner in you to obtain the deeds and machinery and to the ministries that need education and mentorship. Through all the fog created by the brethren, the strange events and happenings in the heaven and on the earth, when it seems like you can't see Him, for sure, you can hear Him! One way to release and alleviate the pressures within the Kingdom atmosphere is through the simple act of obedience to God. His ways are not our ways, but we must *"be patient therefore, brethren, unto the coming of the Lord. Behold, the husbandman waiteth for the precious fruit of the earth, and hath long patience for it. Be ye also patient; stablish your hearts: for the coming of the Lord draweth nigh. Grudge not one against another, brethren."* James 5:7-9 You are not the only one that's going north! You are not the only one that hears! You are not the only one who received the signal. You are not the only one migrating. You are not the only one that has established your heart to write the book, earn the degree/certificate, to say yes to the call, to complete the CD or to open the business. What we have failed to realize is that the phenomena of Kingdom migration is not strange, it's happening throughout the Kingdom rule of God. Migration is not a case of everybody's doing it, she's doing it or he's doing it, it's due to the fact of seasonal disturbance and change. The people of God that have heard and recognized are migrating north, **together**. There's no fighting in migrating, we fly **together**, we land **together**, we take advantage of the land (world) and we keep our families **together**. We come forth in our ministries, write our books, produce our music and open our businesses **together**. The world says, "They will ride **together** and die **together**," but we say, "We fly **together** and live **together**!" And at the coming of the Lord Jesus Christ, we will get caught up, **together**. The will of God will be done and every established heart will have fulfilled their destiny.

2 Deforesting of Kingdom trees:

Deforesting or Deforestation is defined as the clearance of naturally occurring forest. As we have established in chapter IV, namely Horticulture, men are seen as trees. Deuteronomy 20:19-20: Mark 8:22-25 We should not cut down trees certainly not within the Kingdom of God, as they represent men, bring life to those around and show forth the praises of our God. But deforestation is happening anyway within the walls and complex of the Kingdom!

The Bible says, *"Even so the tongue is a little member, and boasteth great things. Behold how great a matter a little fire kindleth! And the tongue is a fire, a world of iniquity: so is the tongue among our members, that it defileth the whole body, and setteth on fire the course of nature; and it is set on fire of hell."* The problem with the freedom of speech is not only seen in the areas of local newspapers, TV media or in general conversation, but a major problem experienced in the body of Christ is the spirit of gossip. Every Christian should be concerned about their freedom of speech. James tells us that the tongue is one of the smallest members but is one of the most dangerous weapons in the entire world. *"But the tongue can no man tame; it is an unruly evil, full of deadly poison."* James 3:8 No zoo keeper or circus master can capture or tame it. This tiny member in the mouth that lives behind the cage of the teeth can ignite a great forest fire with little words unwisely spoken. As we grasp the traveling power of forest fires, the killing of men's souls, we will see its devastating ability to leap from one tree top to another. This small member can create such a fire that can quickly spread leaving absolutely nothing behind; destroying character, ministries, businesses, families, churches and nations.

James tries to bring to mind the weight of influence that comes from this devastating member called the tongue when it is powered by the fire from hell. He says in verse 6 that *"the tongue is a fire, a world of iniquity: so is the tongue among our members, that it defileth the whole body, and setteth on fire the course of nature; and it is set on fire of hell."* James 3:6 My Lord! Beast, birds, serpents and things in the sea can be tamed, *"But the tongue can no man tame; it is an unruly evil, full of deadly poison."*

If you say that you are a member of the Kingdom and you speak the praises of God and can also spue out blasphemies, curses and gossip, does that make you two-faced, double-minded or even forked-tongue as a serpent? For…*"No fountain will bring forth bitter water and sweet water from the same place. Nor can a fig tree bring forth olive berries."* James 3:11-12 Your tongue will reveal the genuine faith that resides within the heart. Every true Kingdom dweller should speak with *"the wisdom that is from above that is first pure, then peaceable, gentle, and easy to be entreated, full of mercy and good fruits, without partiality, and without hypocrisy."* James 3:17

Come out and be ye separated from those that produce pollution into the atmosphere. Let's stop burning each other adding smoke and poison to the places we reside. No longer mingle or mix your faith with the works of iniquity. Solomon writes, *"Death and life are in the power of the tongue: and they that love it shall eat the fruit thereof."* Proverbs 18:21 Love the power of life and the fruit of God and speak only of what digesting His fruit can bring.

These are just two of the many effects that Kingdom dwellers are experiencing. Kingdom answers do not come from the world's systems when God has already given us answers from within Himself. Let's not add to the problem but let's be a part of the solution ready to establish our hearts to produce and speak words of encouragement to our migrating brethren. When we do this we lessen the effects and the penalties of Kingdom Warming.

Kingdom Warming

Exercise: Give a spiritual ideology concerning
The Green House Effect & Global Warming.

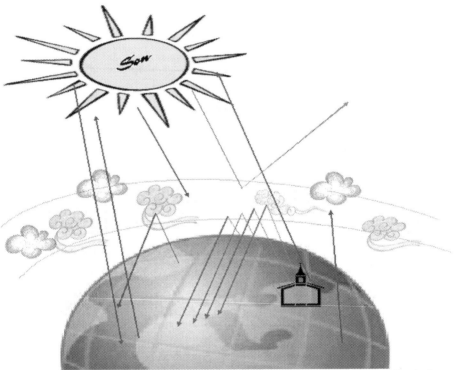

Shows the frequency and increased intensity of natural disasters as due to break down in atmosphere revealing the glory of God in the form of judgment. No one can see God and Live. 1 John 4

Chapter X
Environmental Protection Agency

The Environmental Protection Agency is an independent federal agency established to coordinate programs aimed at reducing pollution and protecting the environment. The concerns of this agency include natural resources, human health, economic growth, energy, transportation, agriculture, industry, and international trade. The EPA was founded in the United States to protect the health of every human and to safeguard the elements of the air, water, and land that they depend on for life. More specifically the agency uses the best available scientific information to make sure that all Americans are protected from any potential harm in the places they live, learn and work. These Federal laws protecting human health and the environment are enforced fairly and effectively. The United States also plays an important leadership role in working with other nations to protect the entire global.

The obvious areas for protecting public health and the environment include the following:

CLEAN AIR: The EPA is charged to make and keep the air in American communities safe and healthy to breathe. This is especially important for the children, the elderly, and people with respiratory ailments. The acts in reducing air pollution will protect the environment and also protect the existing ecosystems.

CLEAN AND SAFE WATER: The EPA is charged to have drinking water that is clean and safe for consumption. Under immediate protection is every river, lake and wet-lands, also included are the coastal and ocean waters able to maintain fish, plants, and wildlife. SAFE FOOD: The EPA is charged to see that all foods are free from unsafe pesticide residues, bacteria and germs. The Food and Drug Administration (FDA) and EPA have issued joint consumer advisories to bring about better awareness and safety to the public.

PREVENTING of POLLUTION: The EPA is charged to cost-effectively prevent pollution by eliminating and reducing harmful emissions and pollutants in the air, resulting in a cleaner and safer environment for all Americans.

WASTE SITES, AND EMERGENCY RESPONSE: The EPA is charged to restore, treat, and dispose of hazardous waste and regular waste preventing harm to Americans and the natural environment. They also respond to emergencies such as chemical spills, oil spills, illegal disposal of chemicals and byproducts detrimental to our air, land and waters.

REDUCTION OF ENVIRONMENTAL RISKS ON BORDERS AND GLOBALLY: The EPA is charged to lead other nations successfully in reducing further stratospheric ozone depletion and other hazards of international concern.

AMERICANS SHOULD HAVE THE RIGHT TO KNOW: The EPA
is charged to inform citizens concerning their local environment.
EPA has along with the Occupational Safety and Health Act (OSHA)
created a list of every hazardous chemical that humans may be
exposed to in all industrial sectors. This was enforced because
everyone needs and has a right to know the hazards and the identities
of chemicals they may be exposed to and what protective measures
are available to prevent any harmful effects they may produce. This
information will give each citizen the tools necessary to protect
themselves, their families and their communities as they see fit.
This information is compiled from scientists, public health officials,
businesses, citizens, and from all levels of government, in hopes
that greater knowledge about the environment will help in earth's
protection.

The United States plays an important role as forerunner of emissions
and pollution clean-up. In fact President Obama has announced
his plans of how the Environmental Protection Agency (EPA) will
regulate industrial greenhouse gas emissions under the Clean Air
Act of 2009-2010.

In the Kingdom of God the Environmental Protection Agency is the
church and should be known as Kingdom Environmental Protection
Agency (K_{EPA}) in the near future. This agency was built on the rock
of Christ that needs no funding as He is the source. The K_{EPA} was
founded on the day of Pentecost to protect the health of man's body,
soul and spirit. It sets the standards through the Word of God that is
declared to the people, published and concealed not. Jeremiah 50:2
The President, Christ, has announced to anyone that is willing to seek
first the Kingdom of God, of His plans to ensure every citizen with

clean life through the Word of God. His proposal includes the areas of natural and spiritual health, prosperity and economic growth of the soul, perfection of gifts, manifestations of fruit of the Spirit, joy and transportation to glory, just to name a few. When the regulations of K_{EPA} are properly adhered to, it protects Spiritual health from any potential harm lurking in the places where citizens may live, learn and work. The church or body of Christ plays a significant part in bringing other members into the knowledge of K_{EPA}.

Let's review the spiritual areas under the protection of the K_{EPA}, they include the following:

CLEAN AIR: The K_{EPA} is charged to keep an atmosphere conducive for the working of the anointing. The breath of God is the sole element that separates the Kingdom dwellers from the creatures of darkness. The Spirit of God is the vehicle by which God speaks to His children and reveals His plan and purpose for their lives. When Kingdom citizens live inhaling and exhaling the breath of God, living a lifestyle that is pleasing to Him, they in turn reduce air pollution protecting themselves and the existing ecosystems.

CLEAN AND SAFE WATER: The K_{EPA} is charged to have water available for baptism. What should prevent a convert from being immediately baptized when they believe? Acts 8:36 Baptism is the outward confession of the conversion that has taken place in the inward parts, it shows that the soul has been transferred from the kingdom of darkness into the Kingdom of Light.

SAFE FOOD: The K_{EPA} is charged to see that only sincere milk, meat and the mysteries of the Word are served from the pulpit and from any forums of Christian education. Every level of Word must be free from tainted doctrine and the philosophies of men. Those serving the Word are to go through rigorous training, learning the culinary skill of serving the Word of God; after which, continuing education should be enforced. The K_{EPA} is not only concerned with good sounding Word but Word that is digested, giving each citizen a chance to produce healthy fruit that will remain.

PREVENTING of POLLUTION: The K_{EPA} is charged to effectively prevent the making of or tolerance of pollutions, from within the church. With the help of prayer, Bible school, church services and pastoral teaching the focus and the mind of the believer is better protected against the wiles of the enemy. By eliminating and reducing harmful emissions of pride, self-righteousness, greed, etc. with the Word of God, the K_{EPA} can help to promote healthy growth among the flock and in turn result in a cleaner and safer environment for all citizens.

WASTE SITES, AND EMERGENCY RESPONSE: The K_{EPA} is charged to treat others as they would like to be treated. Every spiritual employee should be ready to restore such a one that may be overtaken in a fault with the spirit of meekness; considering himself, lest you also be tempted. Galatians 6:1 The K_{EPA} is ready to quickly respond to the cries of the backslider and to encourage them to set aside the weights that would easily beset Hebrews 12:1 as they are of value to the Kingdom of God.

EVERYONE HAS THE RIGHT TO KNOW: The K_{EPA} is charged to inform citizens concerning their reasonable service. Every citizen of the Kingdom of God has the right to know that God is expecting everyone in it to be a part of the Great commission. Every Kingdom dweller is responsible for telling the non kingdom dwellers of the saving grace of Jesus Christ and without Him there will be serious consequences. For the believer to become an over comer, it is also their responsibility to testify of the goodness of God. Every creature of Light and darkness has the right to know who Jesus is and what He has to offer. Everybody ought to know!

In our life time we have experienced one of the greatest disasters the earth has seen, as it affected the air, land and seas, the 2010 oil spill of Bp. This eruption of oil further frustrates the crises of Global Warming. There have been reports of whales, dolphins and large numbers of migrating jelly fish washing up on beaches. The affects of this spill is far from over and yet to be told. This disaster is believed to have happened because the rules and regulations for drilling were not properly been controlled or enforced and no one ever expected such an upset? As man was also given dominion over the fish of the sea, we are responsible for its kingdom. With each passing day, as millions of gallons of oil were pumped into the sea, ocean life was destroyed and that of the livelihoods of those who needed the shores and beached to support their families. There's not enough 뭪AWN to clean up the damage that has been done. As we look within the Kingdom we all can agree that many things have been allowed to go on unchecked, not promptly or justly dealt with. This is the reason for the growing number of dwellers that have little or no fear of the consequences for repeated sins and even less fear of God. But this spill represents the eruption of a spirit coming up from the enemy that cannot easily be cleaned and it will exert it's presence on the air, land and sea in the Kingdom of God.

"Emissions trading" also known as "cap and trade" is an emissions program that the church has adopted seemingly from the other world. Cap and trade is the term used to describe the highest level of emissions allowed in each state, this is called the cap. This program was set in place in hopes of reducing emissions, pollution and poisons from the atmosphere. Many states have complied and have dropped in emitting pollutions, other states have not. The states that have not been successful in reducing their levels of pollution are then allowed to buy the remaining credits from those states that have not capped (out) and have leftover credits for sale. The problem arises when states that cap (out) are then constantly allowed to trade **specific** pollutants, not reducing their emissions, are creating what is called "hotspot." Hotspots can happen within a certain state when many of the known hazardous gases have been effectively reduced except for a certain pollutant. This particular pollutant is the dominating pollutant and is now so concentrated it creates a hotspot. This state is legally allowed to keep buying and trading that pollutant as long as they do not cap out!

This same phenomena is happening within the Kingdom of God. When a local house has mastered the spirit of fornication, theft and patience they however, allow or tolerate other spirits such as greed, lawlessness, perversions, and such the like. When specific spirits are allowed to fester and grow with no restrictions, they can reach levels that are too much, cap. When fellowships, state meetings and national conferences are conducted associations, friendships, networking and trades take place, hence cap and trade. There are many churches, conferences and well known conventions that are known for their hotspots. In the Kingdom of God there are hot spots!!? Hot spots of greed, homosexuality, self righteousness and lewdness have been created.

But God has a remedy for **hot spots**...repentance. REPENT! *"and come out and be ye separated, says the Lord."* 2 Corinthians 6:17 The churches that are lukewarm and the individuals that are lukewarm are most likely the ones given to hot spots because they allow the markets. But there is a way of escape, REPENT and be DELIVERED! God can get you out. Revelation 3:16

When illegal hot spots are allowed, a market for it is also created. When a good movie comes out, remember how the boot legger's would go to the movies and copy it on their personal video recorders and people would still purchase the tape knowing that they would probably hear people talking, eating and see people moving about in the movie theater? Not anymore, today the process is much more sophisticated. The illegal boot legged DVD's are made so well, it looks like they are coming straight from the director's studio and now the market for an illegal and cheaper DVD has grown into a million dollar business! Again when illegal hot spots are allowed in the churches a market for it is also created. John 2:13-17 says, *"And the Jews' Passover was at hand, and Jesus went up to Jerusalem. And found in the temple those that sold oxen and sheep and doves, and the <u>changers</u> of money sitting: And when He had made a scourge of small cords, He drove them all out of the temple, and the sheep, and the oxen; and poured out the changers' money, and overthrew the tables; And said unto them that sold doves, Take these things hence; make not my Father's house an house of <u>merchandise</u>. And His disciples remembered that it was written, the zeal of thine house hath eaten me up."* The word merchandise is the same word used in II Peter 2:1-3 when he talked about how men (leaders) make merchandise of you (to the enemy) when they don't confront you with the truth. When the truth is not proclaimed or enforced, it is as if false doctrine is released instead. But Revelation 18:3, 18 tells us that there is coming a day when the merchandise (selling) of twisted words and false doctrine will no longer be purchased and those that were selling will mourn knowing that their damnation slumbereth not. The merchants of churches who allow usury or this false exchange to go on in the house of God will have to answer to God for all the markets they have created. Markets (or dens) of pride, sex, greed, uncleanness, lasciviousness, idolatry, witchcraft, and such the like that have gone into high demand because of false balances.

It's time to turn over the tables and ask every false seller and changer to take these things away! Every citizen should pray for their leader and become a recruit of the K_{EPA}, because Father God needs you! The Kingdom needs you! We have to protect our Kingdom, everyone can be a part. If Christ has to protect the church to present it one day *"without spot or wrinkle or any such thing... holy and without blemish"* Ephesians 26:27 then likewise every leader must *"preach, warning every man, and teaching every man in all wisdom; that they may present every man perfect in Christ Jesus."*

Colossians 1:28 Then Paul says to the believer, for every person you win to the Kingdom of God, protect them, for they are your *"hope, joy, and crown of rejoicing? Are not even they in the presence of our Lord Jesus Christ at his coming? For they are our glory and joy."* 1 Thessalonians 2

What are you protecting? Father God wants you! Every concerned Kingdom citizen should be ready to protect and die for their Kingdom. It's time to recruit. Be a part of K_{EPA} today.

Father God wants You

Chapter XI
The Feast of Israel

AND ON THE 4ᵀᴴ DAY

*"God said, Let there be lights (stars, the moon) in the firmament of the heaven to divide the day from the night; and let them be for signs, and for **seasons**, and for days, and years."* Genesis 1:13, 14

And let them be for signs and for seasons… means and let them be for "an appointed time."

In the beginning the earth was appointed time and given a place in the galaxy. In the beginning Adam and Eve had an appointed place, in the Garden of Eden and they were given an appointed time, which was in the cool of the evening. God designates appointed times when He request a meeting with **us**. He desires to meet with His people – **<u>Together!</u>** He dictated the dates and proper observances to Moses so that He could meet with His people, **together.** Micah 2:12 is quoted, *"I will surely **assemble**, O Jacob, all of thee; I will surely gather the remnant of Israel; I will put them **together."*** On the day of Pentecost we read in Acts 2:1, *"And when the day of Pentecost was fully come, they were all with one accord in one place."* Hebrews 10:25 says, *"Not to forsake the assembling of ourselves **together**."* Even concerning the coming of the Lord we understand that *"we which are alive and remain shall be caught up* ***together*** *with them in the clouds, to* ***meet*** *the Lord in the   air: and so shall we ever be with the Lord."* <u>1 Thessalonians 4:17</u>

It bothers me and should bother you, when you hear that the saints are not getting along, that the saints are fighting against one another and that strife is among the brethren.

God has set aside an appointed time just for His people. Non-Jewish Bible believers feel the festivals are exclusively Jewish feasts. However, <u>Leviticus 23:1-2, 4</u> tells us very clearly that these are festivals of the Lord and in reality they are for both Jew and non-Jew, to be celebrated jointly with each other. There is a Hebrew word, ger it means stranger in English who has joined himself to the Jewish people. Deuteronomy 16:10-16 The Feasts were given to the people of God and this also includes non-Israeli people who have accepted Him and have been grafted into Israel. As we study the festivals or feast of the Lord, we take notice that they are both historical, as not to forget where God has brought us from and prophetically as it reminds us of where we're going. The feast teaches us about God, His might acts and how our affection of worship should be towards Him, as we grow in the knowledge of Him. These feasts also lay down the background of our Creator's cycle concerning agricultural times of sowing and reaping a harvest.

It is important to remember that each feast and festival also teaches us from start to finish, about the complete plan of God, where each feast centers on a particular plan of God. The seven Feasts of Israel are not just quaint religious festivals of times gone by but they were and still are occasions when God's people pause to remember their history and their God. Each feast will help us understand the character of our God. Each feast provides wonderful essential truths and teachings instructing His people to come to know Him. These feast' represent our past, present and future where Jesus is the fulfillment and will be the final fulfillment in the last stage. He is the Alpha and Omega, the Beginning and the End, the First and the Last.

For the purpose of this chapter, our aim is to explain the natural cycle of seasons as they relate to the agricultural times of sowing and harvesting. Let's peruse the seven feasts of Israel given to Moses in Leviticus 23 for the people of Israel and the times of their observation. Below is a chart that can be used to help follow the Feast, the month and its corresponding times of sowing and reapinging.

The Festivals, the Rains, and the Harvest of the Jewish Nation

Numbers	Jewish Months	Months	Feasts and Events	Sowing & Harvest
1	Nisan	March-April	14th Passover 15th Unleavened Bread	Latter rains Ripening of grain Barley harvest begins
2	Iyar	April-May		Barley harvest completed
3	Sivan	May-June	16th-17th Pentecost. Feast of Weeks, seven weeks after Passover	Dry season Wheat harvest begins
4	Tamuz	June-July		Wheat harvest completed/First figs
5	Av	July-August		Vintage (grape harvest)
6	Elul	August-September		Former or first rains Fruit harvest
7	Tishrei	September-October	1st Jewish New Year-Rosh Hashanna Feast of Trumpets 10th Day of Atonement (Yom Kippur) 15th Feast of Tabernacles (sukkoth)	Gathering of Fruit Plowing begins
8	Cheshvan	October-November		Plowing / grain planting

9	Kislev	November-December		Grain planting continues
10	Teves	December-January	Feast of Lights - Hannukkah celebrates the re-dedication of the Temple in 168 BC.	
11	Shevat	January-February		
12	Adar	February-March	13-14th Purim	Almond in bloom flax harvest

The first feast is The Feast of Passover

The Passover celebrated God's great deliverance of His people from Egyptian slavery. As the death angel came to take away the lives of every first born in Egypt it Passed over the homes of every blood covered door post of the Israelites, spearing their first born and the feast of Passover was birthed. Today, the Passover is a symbol of Jesus Christ our Passover lamb who was sacrificed and died for us that we might apply His blood to our lives escaping the penalty of sin, which is death. The Passover is usually during the months of March and April, and is connected to the harvesting of grains and barley.

The second feast is The Feast of Unleavened Bread

This festival of Unleavened Bread, reminds the Israelites of their need and urgency to leave Egypt quickly, having no time to let their dough rise. During this feast they ate unleavened bread, having no yeast. Bread represents the body or the flesh. Leaven is a symbol of 'puffed up' sin. So during Passover, the people of Israel were to eat unleavened bread made without any yeast whatsoever indicating a sinless life. For the church, this feast symbolizes the need and urgency for the believer to be freed from the oppressions and pollutions of this world and its enslavement to sin and its penalty of death. *"But this I say, brethren, the time is short" we don't have much time. Therefore purge out the old leaven, that you may be a new lump, since you truly are unleavened. For indeed Christ, our Passover, was sacrificed for us, therefore let us keep the feast, not with old leaven, nor with the leaven of malice and wickedness, but with the unleavened bread of sincerity and truth."* 1 Corinthians 5:7, 8 Every believer should live their lives standing ready to escape this life when the leader signals for the troop to move. The Feast of Unleavened Bread is usually during the months of March and April, and is connected to the harvesting of grains, barley and wheat.

The third feast is The Feast of First Fruit

This festival of First Fruit was to thank God for the harvest of food that gave people life. The following Sabbath after the Passover is called the Feast of First Fruits. The people were to bring a sheaf of the first fruits of their harvest to the priest, *"And he shall wave the sheaf before the LORD, to be accepted for you: on the morrow after the Sabbath the priest shall wave it."* Leviticus 23:11 Jesus fulfilled this feast when He rose from the dead on the first day of the week or the Sabbath following the Passover. Thus Resurrection Sunday came on the very day in which the Feast of First fruits had been celebrated! How perfect is that? As this feast applies to the church, we read, *"But now Christ is risen from the dead, and has become the first fruits of those who have fallen asleep. For since by man came death, by man also came the resurrection of the dead. For as in Adam all die, even so in Christ all shall be made alive. But each one in his own order: Christ the first fruits, afterward those who are Christ's at His coming."* 1 Corinthians 15:20-23 At the next coming of Christ He will come to gather the 1ˢᵗ fruit of many brethren to wave before His Father, that you may be accepted. The Feast of First Fruit is usually during the months of March and April, and is connected to the harvesting of wheat.

The fourth feast is The Feast of Weeks (Pentecost Sunday)

"And you shall count to you from the morning after the Sabbath, from the day that you brought the sheaf of the wave offering (Our Easter); seven Sabbaths shall be complete: Even to the morning after the seventh Sabbath you shall number fifty days (Pentecost); and you shall offer a new grain offering to the LORD." This time line is from

Easter to Pentecost. The Hebrew word for "sheaf" is *omer*. An *omer* is defined as "a measure of dry things. Leviticus 23:15-22 In the OT a sheaf was the offering that was waved to the Lord; a sheaf can also represent a person. Example: Joseph told the story of his dream to his brothers, of how during the harvesting season their sheaf bowed down to his sheaf. Well, Genesis 37, 42, 42 and 44 tells us that this dream was prophetic as his family experienced famine in their home land and Joseph was the one, unbeknown, that they had to bow down to for food.

In the NT, we find the fulfillment of this festival in the resurrection of Jesus from the dead. It isn't figurative language being used to speak of Jesus' resurrection but it actually took place on the exact same day as the festival of first fruits, our Easter. Now a new offering was commanded to be waved before God in the Temple. Just like the seed of barley that fell into the earth and brought forth a sheaf, so the seed of Christ's body was sown into the earth and brought forth new life, new power and a new offering. The church will likewise have the same power of the resurrected Savior. Pentecost was the end of one feast and the beginning of something new, the new birth. The church is the new offering to be raised or presented to the Lord *"a glorious church, not having spot, or wrinkle, or any such thing."* Ephesians 5:27 The Feast of Weeks is usually during the months of May and June, and is connected to the dry season and the beginning of wheat harvesting.

The fifth feast is The Feast of Trumpets (called Rosh Hashanah)

Numbers 10:1-2 says, *"And the LORD spake unto Moses, saying, make thee two trumpets of silver; of a whole piece shalt thou make them: that thou mayest use them for the calling of the assembly, and for the journeying of the camps."* One trumpet sound was used to assemble the elders of Israel and the second trumpet was to assemble the whole congregation. It's amazing that God established the use of trumpets to communicate with the leaders and the entire nation, that it's time to come together!!! Even today, we are being spiritually trained to hear distinctive sounds in the atmosphere. We can discern sounds of healings, deliverances and of war. Joel 2:1 says, *"Blow ye the trumpet in Zion, and sound an alarm in my holy mountain: let all the inhabitants of the land tremble: for the day of the LORD cometh, for it is nigh at hand;"* Joel 2:15 says, *"Blow the trumpet in Zion, sanctify a fast, call a solemn assembly:"* God has made each one of his children not only able to hear the sound but to have the capability to sound the alarm using their voice as a trumpet. The preacher's voice is a TRUMPET yes, but God expects every believer to sound the alarm of His coming.

Another symbol of Yahweh's mouth piece is the use of the ram's horn. This trumpet is called the shophar. It is able to make a long and loud distinctive sound when blown. It is our task as the Almighty's mouth piece, to identify Sin - loud and clear! Isaiah 58:1says *"Cry aloud, spare not, lift up thy voice like a trumpet, and shew my people their transgression."* 1 Corinthians 14:8 *"For if the trumpet gives an uncertain sound, who shall prepare himself to the battle?"* Jeremiah 4:19 *"My bowels, my bowel! I am pained at my heart; my heart maketh a noise in me; I cannot hold my peace, because thou hast heard, O my soul, the sound of the trumpet, that alarm of war."* The application of this feast for us today points to the rapture. There is coming a day when the trumpet shall sound from heaven and the Lord will gather all His people unto Himself. 1 Thessalonians 4:16

"For the Lord Himself shall descend from heaven with a shout, with the voice of the archangel, and with the trump of God: and the dead in Christ shall rise first." This feast takes place in September and October when the latter rain comes and the plowing begins.

The sixth feast is The Feast of Atonement (called Yom Kippur)

The Feast of Atonement is the highest of holy days for the Jews and is sometimes called the 'day of awe', held on the tenth day of Tishri (September–October), the first month of the Jewish year. It is a day of fasting, penitence, and cleansing from sin, ending the ten days of penitence that follows Rosh Hashanah. Only one man was busy, and that man was the high priest. Lev 16:30 says, *"For on that day shall the priest make an atonement for you, to cleanse you, that ye may be clean from all your sins before the LORD."* The word "atonement" is used 15 times in Leviticus 16 and it means "to cover." Under the Old Testament economy, the blood of the sacrifices could not put away sin; it could only cover sin. The blood of bulls, lambs and goats could not take away sin; it could only cover sin. It was only through the shed blood of Jesus Christ that would once and for all take away the sins of the world. John 1:29 says, *"The next day John seeth Jesus coming unto him, and saith, Behold the Lamb of God, which taketh away the sin of the world."* Salvation is not by our works, we can do nothing, the Great High priest Jesus, did it all. The annual Day of Atonement speaks to us of God's love and grace. There is nothing we can do. *"Not by works of righteousness which we have done, but according to His mercy He saved us"* Titus 3:5. In the NT Paul writes in Ephesians 5:25-27 saying, *"Husbands, love your wives, even as Christ also loved the church, and gave Himself for it; that He might sanctify and cleanse it with the washing of water by the Word, that*

He might present it to Himself a glorious church, not having spot, or wrinkle, or any such thing; but that it should be holy and without blemish" This feast takes place in September and October when the former rain comes and the plowing begins.

The seventh feast is The Festival of Tabernacles

The word *tabernacle* means "temporary dwellings or abodes" this Feast could also be called "The Feast of Temporary Dwellings." <u>Leviticus 23:40-43</u> tells us that this last and final festival was celebrated after the people had gathered in all their produce of their threshing floor and winepress. This was the most joyous feast of all festive seasons. The people were to celebrate the Festival of Tabernacles on the fifteenth day of the seventh month. It was to last for seven days, full of festivities and worship. The people were to do no work whatsoever. Moses also commanded the people to build sukkoths from branches in the wilderness and for seven days they were to live there and worship the Lord. This Feast was a reminder to the descendants that their ancestors had to live in booths when God delivered them out of Egypt, and it also points to the time when Israel and all nations will be gathered together unto the Lord. The Feast of Tabernacles was God's way to give His people a foretaste of the soon-coming Millennium. They were to approach God for atonement and reconciliation during each of the seven days through the Burnt Offering. (v.36) All the crops had been long stored, all fruits were gathered, the vintage past, and now the land had only to await the softening and refreshment of the 'former rain,' to prepare it for a new crop. *"Be joyful at your Feast: you, your sons and daughters, your menservants and maidservants, and the Levites, <u>the aliens</u>, the fatherless and the widows who live in your towns. For* *seven days celebrate the Feast to the LORD your God at the place the LORD will choose. For the LORD your God will bless you in all your harvest and in all the work of your hands, and your joy will be complete."* Leviticus 23:39-43 The application for us today is seen as we maintain the constant realization that we are sojourners and pilgrims passing through. We must realize that this world is only temporary and that we are on a journey. Abraham focused on *"a city...whose builder and maker is God", "not having received the promises, but having seen them afar off"* prophetically. Hebrews 11:10, 13 God wants to remind the believer that He is the one that led them out of Egypt, (out of sin) and through the wilderness, (the trials of life) and He will continue to be that God unto the promise land (heaven). Just listen and stay focused. The Feast of Tabernacles is a reminder to us that everything we have, (our harvest) everything we are or ever hope to be, comes from God. Everything we have belongs to God, we are just stewards. This feast reminds us that our bodies are the sukkot, frail, flimsy, and temporary, made from the dust of the ground. You were once a wanderer, but now God has prepared a place for you where you can settle down, rest from your labor, cease from troubling and let your soul be at rest. This feast takes place in September and October when the former rain comes and the plowing begins.

Every one of these Feast' depict the incredible plan of God and shows forth many of the pivotal events in the history of the Israelites. In them we see the desire of God for consistent relationship with His people. Every feast is a divinely ordained "time out," to reflect upon our awesome destiny and the purpose for our life, but more importantly for the purpose of this chapter, we see within the feast, how God still holds His occupation in the field of Horticulture that shows us the order and cycle for productivity in the Kingdom.

The Kingdom of God and its dwellers are about to bring the greatest re-education program of productivity the world has ever seen and we all have an opportunity to be part of it. The order of production is this: obey God, sow into the earth, watch Him send the rain, till or work the ground and He will bring the increase." Let the Kingdom teach the world.

Chapter XII
Due Season

Concerning the children of Israel in the O.T. God instructed them to celebrate the seven feast, all of which were directly or indirectly related to the times and seasons of **Agriculture.** These feast' were tremendous depictions of God's abundance as He provides for His people. God's people can experience the perfect conditions needed for the success of their planting, harvesting and livelihoods through their obedience towards God. An abundant harvest was a cause for great rejoicing. The three major Feast seasons were tied to the harvest times of Israel as stated in the previous Chapter. **Barley**, the first of the grains, from this feast came the Waving of the Sheaf Offering, which happens in the spring from March-April to May. This also coincides with the Feast of Unleavened Bread and the harvesting of **wheat** in late spring-early summer from May through to June-July, marking the time of Pentecost, the Feast of Weeks. Then we have the summer **fruits**: olives, dates, figs and grapes harvested from August to September, with the latter feast coming to an end with the Feast of Trumpets, Feast of Atonement and Feast of Tabernacles.

The seven months from March to about October were filled with the sowing and harvesting of the land with the remaining portion of the year used mainly to cultivate and manicure the land.

The streams with their minerals from the mountains made the soil of Palestine rich for cultivation. Psalms 1:3; 65:10; Proverbs 21:1; Isaiah 30:25; 32:2, 20; Hosea 12:11 The farmers also understood that by applying manure to the soil it added more fertility to the earth. The soil was so rich to such the degree, that in the days of Solomon there was an abundance like this: 20,000 measures of wheat year by year were sent to Hiram in exchange for timber 1 Kings 5:11 large quantities of wheat were sent to the Tyrians as trade Ezekiel 27:17 the wheat sometimes produced an hundredfold Genesis 26:12; Matthew 13:23 figs and pomegranates were very plentiful Numbers 13:23, and the vine and the olive tree grew abundantly Deuteronomy 33:24.

Water drops that fall as precipitation from clouds is what we call rain. In any given day we can experience heavy rain, moderate rain or light rain. In the Bible we read about early rain, former rain, first rain or latter rain. The water supply for vegetation in Egypt was supplied mostly by the Nile River. However in Palestine, Canaan the promise land, there were no oceans or rivers to rely or depend on. The people had to depend solely on the rain that fell from heaven. The rains were seriously needed for themselves, the animals and for planting. The children of Israel were told by Moses that they would go to a land which *"drinketh water of the rain of heaven"* this meant that the land would never go dry because of the abundance of rain. Deuteronomy 11:11 There were many wells found in the valleys, but their existence depended directly on the rain fall or snow run off from the mountains. So, for the people of Israel, the rains in these dry lands were essential for sowing in the spring and reaping in the fall seasons. The failure of rain fall at the proper times or a change in the amount of rain was of great concern when considering the economy of the nation.

The promise of prosperity is given to the people in the form of the "abundance of rain" and "rain in due season" Leviticus 26:4 It was always God's good pleasure to bless His people. *"And the LORD shall make thee plenteous in goods, in the fruit of thy body, and in the fruit of thy cattle, and in the fruit of thy ground, in the land which the LORD sware unto thy fathers to give thee. The LORD shall open unto thee His good treasure, the heaven to give the rain unto thy land in his season, and to bless all the work of thine hand: and thou shalt lend unto many nations, and thou shalt not borrow."* Deuteronomy 28:11, 12 This was the blessing for the obedient children of the Father.

But, any time the children of Israel got out of line, stiff necked or disobedient, their blessings of rains were threatened. The Lord would say through Moses, *"Take heed to yourselves, that your heart be not deceived, and ye turn aside, and serve other gods, and worship them; and then the LORD's wrath be kindled against you, and He shut up the heaven, that there be no rain, and that the land yield not her fruit; and lest ye perish quickly from off the good land which the LORD giveth you."* *"I will surely consume them, saith the LORD: there shall be no grapes on the vine, nor figs on the fig tree, and the leaf shall fade; and the things that I have given them shall pass away from them."* *"When the heaven is shut up, and there is no rain, because they have sinned against thee; yet if they pray toward this place, and confess thy name, and turn from their sin, when thou dost afflict them; then hear thou from heaven, and forgive the sin of thy servants and of thy people Israel..."* Deuteronomy 11:16, 17, Jeremiah 8:13, Chronicles 6:26, 27a The withholding of rain according to the prophecy of Elijah caused the mountain streams to dry up, and a certain famine was issued. A glimpse of this terrible suffering from the lack of rain water is given to us to see the hand of God at the disobedience of His chosen. The people were uncertain of another meal 1 Kings 17:1-12 and the animals were perishing 1 Kings 18:5.

From the beginning, the blessing was upon the ground as man continued in obedience, but when Adam sinned, the Lord declared, *"And unto Adam He said, Because thou hast hearkened unto the voice of thy wife, and hast eaten of the tree, of which I commanded thee, saying, Thou shalt not eat of it: cursed is the ground for thy sake; in sorrow shalt thou eat of it all the days of thy life; thorns also and thistles shall it bring forth to thee; and thou shalt eat the herb of the field; in the sweat of thy face shalt thou eat bread, till thou return unto the ground; for out of it wast thou taken: for dust thou art, and unto dust shalt thou return."* Genesis 3:17-19

During the harvesting times, wheat, grapes and olives were the major crops produced in the land of Philistine. It was very important to the economy of Israel that the rains came at the appropriate times. The rains for consideration were the former rains followed by the latter rains. The former or the 1st rains prepared the ground for what was going into it and the latter rains grew whatever had been planted. *"And it shall come to pass, if ye shall hearken diligently unto my commandments which I command you this day, to love the LORD your God, and to serve Him with all your heart and with all your soul, that I will give you the rain of your land in his due season, the first rain* (autum season) *and the latter rain* (spring season), *that thou mayest gather in thy corn (barley), and thy wine, and thine oil."* Deuteronomy 11:13, 14

From the scriptures we understand that the former or first rains during these Palestinian times fell just before sowing-time. This rain was necessary to ensure germination of the seed for growth. Under the influence of the fertilizing showers, the tender shoot springs up. Mark 4:29 sets the order, *"For the earth bringeth forth fruit of herself; first the blade, then the ear, after that the full corn in the ear."* The Latter rains came to ensure that what was put in the ground could now grow with increase and yield an increase. As long as the children of God obeyed the will of God, the cycle continued unbroken: obey... rain, disobey...famine.

For the believer, however we understand from N.T. scripture that the early rains seems to represent the time of Passover & Pentecost as we see the out pouring of the Holy Spirit, at the birth of the church. This was followed by the rainy season or shower seasons where the church began to grow, gain strength and become a recognized power. The church also experienced the showers of rain through times of revivals that came now and then.

SIDE BAR: Moreover, today it seems as if the church, the body of Christ, is not growing, has no strength and is a joke to the world. Could it be from the lack of rain or perhaps from some spiritual type of palmerworms, locusts, caterpillar or cankerworm? If this is so, should we bother asking God to send the latter rain or should we ask God to send us the former rains again? Should we do our first works over?

There is no need to look for the latter rain when the grounds have not been ploughed, turned over or broken up. We must break up the fallow ground! Fallow ground is an area, plot or a lot of land that was once used for agriculture bearing much fruit but has since been un-worked, left hard and is now full of dead roots, yielding nothing. This is what happens when the church grows cold and is not doing the will of God. This is also the perfect picture of many churches, America and numerous of Christians therein, today. The believer must begin to sow the Word: A sower went out to sow his seed... The seed is the Word of God.   Luke 8 The believer must begin to sow to themselves: *"Sow to yourselves in righteousness and reap in mercy."* Hosea 10:12

In the midst of all that is happening, in the natural world and in the Kingdom of God, it still remains, that God wants to restore His people. Many have begun plowing their land, many have broken up their fallow ground and many have already planted their seeds because they have heard the command in the atmosphere saying, "It's time to work, it's time to plow and it's time to sow, bring Forth!" Those that have sown may have experienced the former rain and are now awaiting and eligible to receive the next phase of the cycle, the promised latter rain.

The latter rain is only profitable to those who have plowed the ground of their own souls and spirits, bundled and burned the weeds in their lives, up rooted the sins that so easily besets or broken the strong hold of the enemy. The latter rain is coming! But it is coming only to those who have DONE something, even in their dry seasons, which is always part of the cycle!!! Some Kingdom dwellers have planted in the areas of ministries, business, talents, gifting, government, science, education, economics and entertainment; seeds that will bring increase to the Kingdom. There are some in the Kingdom that are waiting for the latter rain legally!

As we revisit global warming with its uncertain skies, during any given season the weather may not exhibit that season. If you would bring to memory the literal season you are in right now as you read this book, the calendar may show that it is winter, but the weather may exhibit spring time. Likewise, what God is about to do for those that are ready, He is going to send the weather and climate conducive to your seed no matter what the season is, no matter what others are doing and no matter what the trend may be. At any time without a shadow of doubt you can declare, "It's MY season!" Yes God. Be careful not to rely on the weather reports or climate controls of another as their seasons may or may not be in sync with what God is doing for you.

We are living in a time where God is not just adding or multiplying, but He is creating synergistic effects where the sum of what's put together far exceeds the expectations of the sower. Not only will the two rainy seasons overlap, not only will the seasons overlap but the occupations of the sower and the reaper whose jobs reside within two different seasons, God is going to allow their work schedules to overlap causing them to work in the same seasons. Read Amos 9:13 where he declares, *"Behold, the days come, saith the LORD, that the plowman shall overtake the reaper, and the treader of grapes him that soweth seed."* During the uncertainty and disbelief of Kingdom warming, God has a way of fulfilling His Word.

What the prophet Amos is saying to the Kingdom dwellers is to get ready for the overlapping seasons along with their overlapping times of rain and overlapping of harvest times. Yes God. While you are sowing one thing, you will begin reaping a harvest of something else!

Can you imagine God sending your seed the former and the latter rain at the same time? What a synergistic harvest it will bring!!!

Even as we experience Kingdom warming, with its spiritual pollution, uncertain skies and uncharted effects, God is raining down on those that are in their due season. The next time a message goes forth and the messenger request that you declare to your neighbor "it is MY season", please ask yourself if you have done anything to merit a harvest. Have you plowed, have you sown, have you pluck up…what have you done? Yes, we want to receive our W.D., we want to hear Him say well DONE, but the prefix of DONE is DO. What have you done to receive a reward?

In the story of the Fig tree of Mark 11:12-24, verse *12* begins, *"And on the morrow, when they were come from Bethany, He was hungry: And seeing a fig tree afar off having leaves, He came, if haply He might find anything thereon: and when He came to it, He found nothing but leaves; for the time of figs was not yet. And Jesus answered and said unto it, No man eat fruit of thee hereafter forever. And His disciples heard it. Verse 20 And in the morning, as they passed by, they saw the fig tree dried up from the roots. (they were going back to Jerusalem) And Peter calling to remembrance saith unto Him, Master, behold, the fig tree which thou cursedst is withered away. And Jesus answering saith unto them, Have faith in God. For verily I say unto you, That whosoever shall say unto this mountain, Be thou removed, and be thou cast into the sea; and shall not doubt in his heart, but shall believe that those things which he saith shall come to pass; he shall have whatsoever he saith. Therefore I say unto you, what things so ever ye desire, when ye pray, believe that ye receive them, and ye shall have them."*

We have established in chapter 4 that trees can also represent men. We can only imagine that when Jesus came within reach of the tree the first thing Jesus could have said to it was a question, "Why have you not produced any fruit?" And the tree truthfully could reply, "Because it is not MY season." In verse 22 we experience this unheard conversation and Jesus goes on to <u>answer</u> (KJV) the tree *"No man eat fruit of **thee** hereafter forever."* Later Jesus is reminded by one of His disciples of the cruse He pronounced on this now dried up fig tree. Mark 11:15 -24 But, He tells the disciples in response, that they must, *"Have faith!"* What? It would seem to be very unfair that the all knowing Jesus Christ would approach the tree knowing that figs were not in season and then curse the tree for not bearing fruit!!! This passage of scripture like all others is given for instruction and we must realize some of the things Jesus was trying to convey to His disciple and to us today. Opportunities, open doors, or the call of God, none of which wait for seasons! You are to preach, if that's what your seed is, in season and out of season. 2 Timothy 3:16 You are to produce books, if that's what your seed is called to do, in season and out of season. You are to produce songs, helps, businesses, mercy, daycares, plays, CD's, etc., if that's what your seed is called to do, in season and out of season!!! If Bill Gates can change the climate and season of the computer age, which we're still in, then the people of God should experience similar phenomena's. Don't be this fig tree that seemingly was doing everything right; in the right soil, in the right place of opportunity, having the right amount of leaves but no faith to call its fruit into season. Faith will call your seed into season. Faith will make "now" your season. The unprofitable servant who was given the one talent had everything that he needed to produce but he produced nothing. He had no faith in the God that gave him the talent neither in himself. Matthew 25:14-30, Hebrews

11:6 Without faith it is impossible to please God neither can you produce for Him. Every believer must realize that it doesn't matter what the season says on the calendar or the seasons that others may be experiencing, you are responsible to mix works with unwavering faith in God and produce fruit in season and out of season ready for opportunity. Christ also wants His people to recognize and be aware of His coming like a thief in the night. He already knows them that are His, but He's coming; be ye also ready!

"Death and life are in the power of the tongue: and they that love it shall eat the fruit thereof." Proverbs 18:21 We are admonished in chapter 4 to choose life. If we love life, we should speak life and therefore we can eat life. Jesus said to His disciples, *"Have Faith"* then He gives us the example that we can speak to problems and command them to leave. When obstacles are eradicated they make pathways for the things we desire to come forth, therefore, *"he shall **have** whatsoever he saith."* Faith can speak to the removal of any obstacle, problem and demonic influence so that the things desired can now be commanded to come to pass.

As you would take the time in prayer as the watchmen on the wall in the Spirit, you will notice the growing cloud of rain in the atmosphere. 1 Kings 18:43-45 gives us an example of this occurrence where we read, *"And said to his servant, Go up now, look toward the sea. And he went up, and looked...And he said, go again seven times. And it came to pass at the seventh time, that he said, Behold, there ariseth a little cloud out of the sea, like a man's hand...and there was a great rain."*

What God is about to do will not only be a fulfillment for the corporate Kingdom church but also for Kingdom dwellers.

Joel 2 verse 24 says, *"and the floors shall be full of wheat, and the vats shall overflow with wine and oil..."* There can be no mistake that this interpretation is for literal Zion as it also points to the Kingdom of God. The wheat represents the souls that are saved by grace in the parables of the sower. The wine and oil as always represent the joy and healing of the Holy Spirit. To the individual dwellers that are in their due season, get ready to see your *"floors full of wheat, and the vats shall overflow with wine and oil."* As the wheat harvest is the direct result of the latter rains and the wine and oil is the direct result of the former rains, from this prophecy we understand the reconfirmation of God's Word that the rains will happen together.

The product of this rain will come from the seed(s) that the Kingdom dwellers have planted. What have you planted in the Kingdom? Was it a business, an idea, a church, a ministry, a witty invention, or a million dollar business?

In the midst of Kingdom warming where the seasons are visible out of sync, keep the faith in the Word of God. Listen for His voice, He is speaking in the atmosphere and there is but one. It is the same atmosphere where we see the struggles between the angels of Light and the angels of darkness who are laying in wait to hold up your prayers and answers. It is in the same atmosphere that God speaks and many will hear. The response of the hearer depends on their level of relationship and obedience. God is calling forth books, ministries, businesses, innovative ideals, churches, witty inventions, worship, music, revelations, corporations, and so much more from

His people. Many will hear Him and quickly move in obedience to His call. Many will begin to sow and work their seeds, knowing that He will bring the increase. He will bring the increase to the business, to the church, to that ideal, etc. but the Kingdom dweller must move quickly because seasons do change.

Receive your due season. Your due season is the season that comes just before the latter rains, when everything there is to do **has** been done. You have been obedient, you have heard the voice of God in the atmosphere, you have turned your soil, you have planted with faith what He has given you, you have worked that seed, gathered all the information needed for germination and now you are waiting for the latter rains that brings a harvest and increase. You are now in your due season, ready to show forth the Kingdom of God.

"Remember not the former things, neither consider the things of old. Behold, I do a new thing and now it shall spring forth, shall you not know it? I will even make a way in the wilderness and rivers in the desert. The beast of the field shall honor me and the dragons and the owls because I give waters in the wilderness and rivers in the desert to give drink to my people, my chosen. These people have I formed for myself, they shall show forth my praise." Isaiah 43:18, 19

Kingdom warming is a condition that was created by the brothers and sisters within the Kingdom of God but its effects will not affect the due season that God has for His prepared and waiting dwellers.

Suggested

Books for Growth

Kingdom Industrial Revolution
I know my giftings, talents and fruit workbook
Sheila Kelly

"Me" at a Glance
I know who I am workbook
Sheila Kelly

Grow Your Church
FROM INSIDE OUT
Sheila Kelly

The FAITH Reaction
Le Var Kelly

The God We Worship
Joseph N. Williams